WINNING THE PEACE
IN THE PACIFIC

THE MACMILLAN COMPANY
NEW YORK · BOSTON · CHICAGO
DALLAS · ATLANTA · SAN FRANCISCO

MACMILLAN AND CO., LIMITED
LONDON · BOMBAY · CALCUTTA
MADRAS · MELBOURNE

**THE MACMILLAN COMPANY
OF CANADA, LIMITED**
TORONTO

WINNING THE PEACE
IN THE PACIFIC

*A Chinese View of Far Eastern Postwar Plans and
Requirements for a Stable Security System
in the Pacific Area*

By S. R. CHOW

*Professor of International Law,
National Wuhan University. Member of the
People's Political Council, Chungking*

With a Foreword by
Hu Shih

Published in cooperation with the International Secretariat
Institute of Pacific Relations

New York
The Macmillan Company
1944

FOREWORD

As a Chinese member and former officer of the Institute of Pacific Relations, I feel very grateful to the International Secretariat of the Institute for publishing this little book *Winning the Peace in the Pacific* by my old friend, Professor S. R. Chow. In doing so, the Institute is performing a useful service of rectifying an unfortunate situation in present-day international thinking, wherein practically all books and articles on post-war planning and peace problems have come from Anglo-Saxon writers or European scholars in exile, but almost none from Chinese authors. This dearth of authentic presentation of Chinese attitudes and aspirations regarding the post-war world in general or the more specific problems of the peace structure in the Pacific region, has created the erroneous impression that China is still too deeply engrossed in her hard and little-aided war to be able to think about the post-war problems and to present any definitive program for public discussion by the people of the United Nations. And because China has not told the outside world what she has been thinking about these problems, much of the current writing on post-war problems has suffered from the fact that too little attention has been paid to the peace objectives of the Chinese people.

It is to correct this situation and to awaken a new interest of the American and British public in what the Chinese people have been thinking on these important problems that the Institute of Pacific Relations is sponsoring the publication of the views of a thoughtful and forward-looking Chinese scholar who, though not speaking in any sense for the National Government of China, nevertheless best reflects the desires and hopes of a great many of China's intellectual leaders.

Professor Chow, better known in China as Chou Kengsheng, is very well qualified for the task of studying and discussing the problems of post-war planning in the Pacific from a Chinese standpoint. As a student, he spent five years in Japan, five years in England and Scotland and three years in France. He was in England during the First World War and in Paris at the time of the Peace Conference. He taught international law and international relations in three Chinese national universities in the interval between two world wars. He was a victim of Japan's war in China, lost all his books and other earthly possessions by Japanese bombing, and followed his university into exile. He was a Chinese delegate to the I.P.R. Conference at Virginia Beach (1939) and Mont Tremblant (1942). Since October 1939, he has been staying in the United States, making a special study of the war and international problems after the war.

Ever since his student days, he has been a warm admirer of the democratic institutions and ways of life of Great Britain, the United States and the democracies of Western Europe. His scholarship, political independence and intellectual integrity have won him the high respect of Chinese government leaders as well as of the Chinese student world. Very few Chinese scholars are so well equipped by long residence abroad and conscientious training in international thinking as Professor Chow to undertake to write the first book on what the Chinese people want to see set up in the Pacific area when this terrible war is over.

Professor Chow, of course, does not expect that his readers will agree with him on all the points in his peace program for the Pacific. Although he was my house guest in Washington for nearly three years and he and I had almost daily chats on various problems of war and peace, we do not agree, for instance, on his proposal of a regional organization for the Pacific. Personally I do not think such a regional agency is necessary. In the first place, I believe there are no "purely regional problems" which should require so elaborate a regional organization as is outlined in Professor Chow's book. Secondly, it seems to me that the duplication of function and conflict of jurisdiction between the regional agency and the new world organization would surely lead to endless confusion and unnecessary waste. Thirdly, such matters as "a regional system of general security," "economic and military sanctions," and the "control" of a "permanent international military force" can certainly be more adequately planned and administered by a world-wide organization than by any regional agency. Therefore it would seem to me more desirable for the post-war world to devote its first labors to the establishment and implementation of a "world order" which shall afford to all nations and all regions an effective system of general or collective security rather than to attempt to set up some regional authority intermediate between the nations and a world-wide international order. I cite this example only to show that there is plenty of room for discussion and debate on any such program of Far Eastern post-war settlement. And it is fruitful discussion and criticism which, I am sure, the author most earnestly desires to elicit by presenting the results of his own studies and reflections.

HU SHIH

New York
June 1943

EDITORIAL NOTE

The principal aim of the I.P.R. Secretariat in publishing this booklet is well explained in the foreword by Dr. Hu Shih. It should be noted in addition, however, that Dr. Chow has performed the useful service of critically analyzing a number of other studies on related topics, including several documents submitted to the Mont Tremblant Conference of the I.P.R. in December 1942. The booklet is an outgrowth and enlargement of Professor Chow's paper, "A Permanent Order for the Pacific," submitted to that Conference. It should also be noted that certain sections of the study formed the basis of a shorter article published in the October 1942 issue of *Foreign Affairs*. To the editors of that journal the I.P.R. Secretariat and the author are indebted for permission to use those sections. Though the present booklet is issued under the auspices of the International Secretariat of the I.P.R., it should be emphasized that neither the Secretariat nor the National Councils of the I.P.R. assume any responsibility for statements of fact or opinion expressed in the study; for these the author alone is responsible.

W. L. HOLLAND
Research Secretary

New York
June 1943

TABLE OF CONTENTS

xi

WINNING THE PEACE
IN THE PACIFIC

INTRODUCTION

The establishment of a permanent order for the Pacific region is a vast problem in which many complicated issues are involved. In this study no attempt is made to do peace planning in its true sense. I am simply offering suggestions with a view to clarifying the main issues involved so as to facilitate the eventual task of planning by the United Nations statesmen and diplomats at the end of the war. The following sections are mainly concerned with broad principles; a good many details are left to be filled in, especially in that part which deals with the scheme of regional organization.

In dealing with the problem of the postwar Pacific order we have necessarily to begin with a few basic assumptions. First of all, we assume that the United Nations will win the war and the Japanese will be driven out of China and the other countries of the Pacific region which they have invaded. It is also assumed that after the war America will not return to isolationism in its attitude toward world politics, but will, on the contrary, be prepared to share with other great powers the all-important responsibility of building an effective system of collective security for the world. Furthermore, we assume that the Soviet Union, despite its difference from western democracies in political ideology, will fully co-operate with the latter in a common effort for assuring a lasting peace in the postwar world. These are generally considered the basic conditions without whose fulfillment no large scheme for international peace will have a chance to be effective.

CHAPTER I

THE GENERAL PROBLEM

Among the people of the United Nations, there may be considerable differences of opinion about the causes of the present world war, yet most will agree that something must be done for the postwar world order so that the same catastrophe may not befall mankind again, at least in our time. The task is so urgent that we must give it serious attention even while the fighting is still going on.

There are persons who object on various grounds to peace planning in the midst of the war. One objection is that the shape of postwar world order will depend largely upon the outcome of the war: and since this is now still uncertain, there is practically no real basis on which to devise a new order. But it must be understood that plans concerning postwar settlement can only be based upon the assumption, as pointed out above, that the United Nations will completely win the war. Another objection is that the United Nations have to concentrate all their efforts upon winning the war and cannot afford to let the work of peace planning divert their attention from that very urgent task. To this objection we can simply answer that peace planning itself may be considered part of the war effort, considering that to indicate the road to a better world will be a stimulant to popular enthusiasm and effort for winning the war. Again, some contend that discussions of postwar problems in the midst of war might give rise to serious controversies among the United Nations which would impede the prosecution of the war. In reply we can say that, as many complicated and important issues are involved in postwar settlements, these would inevitably give rise to controversies among the United Nations sooner or later. Indeed it is better to see such controversies arise during the war rather than at its end. Inter-allied controversies in the midst of the war would not result in the breaking up of the bond of the United Nations who are bound to stand together against the Axis Powers; while at the end of the war separate national interests may drive nations to take an uncompromising attitude in controversies even at the risk of a rupture. Moreover, once the fighting is ended, many issues will call for *immediate* settlement and then there will be very little time to think out appropriate measures to meet the needs. It is necessary to start peace planning in advance of an armistice or peace conference in order that we may not be caught unprepared for making peace as we were last time. Indeed an early start will have the additional advantage of helping to create an informed world opinion which is essential for carrying out any farreaching constructive schemes in the face of possible strong nationalistic opposition. As Messrs. Herbert Hoover and Hugh Gibson have pointed out in their timely book *The Problem of Lasting Peace* (page 3), there must be just as much preparedness for peace-making as there is for war, and in many ways the preparations for peace are more difficult a task.

It is fitting that far-sighted persons on the side of the United Nations, especially in America, both in government service and outside, are now planning seriously for a better world order after the war. But in doing this we must recognize that no lasting peace is possible for the postwar world without achieving a durable settlement in the Pacific. In his radio address of December 9, 1941, two days after the Japanese attack on Pearl Harbor, President Roosevelt enumerated a series of acts of aggression committed successively by Japan and her Axis partners for the past ten years, beginning with Japan's invasion of China's three Eastern Provinces (generally known as Manchuria) in 1931. The significance of this enumeration was apparent. It was really Japan which started the second World War ten years ago; and it was the failure of the League of Nations—and, to a lesser extent, of the United States—to curb Japanese aggression in the Far East which encouraged the European aggressors to go ahead with their audacious design for world domination. It is no exaggeration to say that the present world war really dates from 1931, the year when the Japanese militarists embarked upon their long-planned war of conquest in the Far East. There is ample past experience to convince us that the shape of the postwar Pacific Order will greatly determine the world order after the war. It may also be pointed out that the problem of peace in the Pacific is complicated by special political, economic, racial and national issues which the war has either raised or aggravated. Settlement of these issues in a manner to promote the interests of the Pacific region as a whole will probably require a regional understanding to be worked out through permanent agencies. Moreover, from the viewpoint of political strategy, the fact that the United Nations are actually planning for a permanent order for the Pacific area once victory is won should serve to counteract Japanese propaganda for a "Greater East Asia Co-Prosperity Sphere" or whatever else the Japanese imperialists may call it, and rally the native peoples of the region to fight the common battle for freedom.

To assure a lasting peace either in a region or for the world as a whole it is always essential, first of all, to make a supreme effort towards eliminating all causes of conflict or friction in international relationship as well as towards checking all vicious forces which make for war. This may be done both during the war and after the end of the war. Then once a peace settlement has been made, there must be provision for some international machinery to assure such international cooperation and collective security as will enable all nations, great or small, to live each in a state of peace and progress. As far as the Pacific region is concerned, four essential requirements must be met before a permanent order can be built.

First, Japan must be completely disarmed after her defeat in the war. Second, there must be a fundamental readjustment in the relationship of China to other powers. Third, the racial and national problems of the region must be solved equitably. Fourth, a regional organization must be formed to establish security and maintain peace.

Limits of space do not permit going into detail on all those points. The first three points are considered only briefly; on the fourth, a more detailed treatment will be attempted.

CHAPTER II

THE TREATMENT OF JAPAN

"The first order of business in framing the peace," as a well-known authority on the Far East observed, "is to deal with Japan."[1] There is almost a unanimous opinion that unless Japan, the age-long aggressor nation in the Far East, is eliminated as a potent force this time, there is no hope of peace in the Pacific region and therefore in the rest of the world. But in order to bring about the desired end, a mere defeat, however crushing it may be, will not be sufficient: Japan must further be completely disarmed after the war. The principle of the disarmament of aggressor nations has already been proclaimed by President Roosevelt and Prime Minister Churchill in the Atlantic Charter, whose eighth point states that, pending the establishment of a permanent system of general security, such disarmament is essential. In a paper read at the annual meeting of the American Political Science Association in New York on December 31, 1941, Dr. Hu Shih, then Chinese Ambassador in the United States, applied this principle specifically to the Far East by stating that the Chinese Government would give full support to the disarming of Japan as one of the necessary factors in the maintenance of peace in the Pacific area.[2] The way in which the Far Eastern crisis has developed during the past twelve years should have convinced the world that

[1] Nathaniel Peffer, *Basis for Peace in the Far East,* New York, 1942.
[2] Reproduced in *Two Papers on Postwar Asia.* China Council Paper No. 1. Institute of Pacific Relations Conference, Mont Tremblant, 1942.

Japan's aggressive policy is a constant menace to the security of neighboring countries. Her military caste is so powerful that it exercises full control over national policy, and its spirit is so extremely nationalistic and chauvinistic that national policy, in turn, is bound to take the form of aggressive territorial expansion. If Japan retains her military superiority there will be little possibility of lasting peace in the Pacific region.

Military and Naval Disarmament

The only effective way to hold Japanese militarism in check is to disarm the country completely. Japan's air and naval forces should be liquidated except for a limited number of small warships which she might be allowed to retain for use by her police and customs services. The remaining Japanese fleet must be surrendered to the United Nations. As a matter of fact, it is not impossible that the very navy of which the Japanese are so proud may be by that time, as some would predict, "largely at the bottom of the sea." In that case, the problem of Japanese naval disarmament would be much simplified. Further, as a measure of air disarmament, the United Nations should take over all aircraft, whether military or non-military, in Japanese possession. Thereafter no military planes should be produced or possessed by Japan. Naval shipbuilding works and munition factories should either be closed down altogether or reduced in number and size to the point at which they will be just sufficient to fulfill agreed peacetime purposes. Land forces should be strictly limited to the number necessary to maintain internal order. Details of the extent and process of Japanese disarmament must be left for experts to work out when the armistice comes. What is essential is that it should be thorough and effective and that any limited armament allowed Japan should be closely supervised by a permament international commission.

To prevent Japan from rearming, such an international commission should, at least temporarily, set up agencies to inspect and investigate Japanese armaments continuously on the spot. Naval and air bases in Japan which are apparently designed for offense should be demolished forthwith. At least until a general plan of world disarmament is adopted, the importation into Japan of arms and ammunition, including military planes, should be completely banned. In addition an efficient control of the sale to Japan of strategical minerals and other raw materials essential for war industry should be established, as Dr. Hu Shih has pointed out, as another method for the prevention of Japanese rearmament.[3] Severe penalties should be set for the violation of any of the disarmament clauses prescribed by the United Nations as a condition of armistice. During the armistice period, or for as long as is necessary to insure Japan's strict observance, the United Nations or whatever world association may be established by them should police Japan by stationing a strong international force at a few strategic points in the Japanese homeland. Prolonged and strict observance of the disarmament clauses by Japan should be a basic condition for her admission into a regional or world association of nations.

It may be contended that the Japanese are a proud and patriotic people who will never bear national humiliation or submit to harsh terms imposed by foreign powers without proportionately increasing their chauvinism and hostility towards foreigners; and that as a result it would be unwise for the United Nations to impose disarmament on a defeated Japan, to set up an international commis-

[3] *Ibid.*

sion to supervise her armaments or to assign an inter-national force to police the country. It might be argued that, on the contrary, a policy of moderation and gen-erosity would help to pacify the Japanese and reconcile them with their former enemies. In my opinion, this viewpoint is both erroneous and dangerous.

Events have fully demonstrated the futility of an ap-peasement policy such as the United States followed to-wards Japan up to the outbreak of war. The Japanese, although capable of extreme fanaticism in individual actions, are complete realists in international relations. A big stick counts with them more than lofty principles, good faith and soft words. It is a mistake to think that one could make the Japanese quiet, reasonable or peace-loving by treating them generously after the war. Their long series of military successes, their great territorial con-quests and the consequent rapid growth of their national power in the past fifty years have developed among them a legend of invincibility. This forms the psychological background of their extreme militarism and ruthlessness. Only thoroughgoing disarmament after a crushing mili-tary defeat can smash that false legend and so help to loosen the traditional grip of the military caste upon the Japanese people. Many informed students of Far Eastern affairs hold a similar view. For instance, Mr. Hallett Abend in his latest book has said:

"The defeat of Japan must also involve the absolute crush-ing of her power to assume the role of the aggressor for at least the next twenty-five years. Thus far the Japanese Empire has never known defeat in any of the wars it has fought in modern times nor have the people known warfare on her own soil. Each war has brought victory, enrichment, elation, and an enhancement of the prestige of the military caste. This war must end in the bitter lesson that international banditry brings fearful punishments. The terrible patriots of Nippon

must be forced to give up the fruits of fifty years of pred-
atory policies, not as a measure of punitive peace, but
primarily as a deterrent against a revival of greedy militarism and as the minimum of the overdue justice owed to
long-suffering China and Korea."[4]

Vice-President Wallace holds a similar and even
stronger view:

"Revenge for the sake of revenge would be a sign of barbar-
ism—but this time we must make absolutely sure that the
guilty leaders are punished, that the defeated nation realizes
its defeat and is not permitted to rearm. The United Nations
must back up the military disarmament with psychological
disarmament—supervision, or at least inspection, of the
school systems of Germany and Japan to undo so far as possible the diabolical work of Hitler and the Japanese war
lords in poisoning the minds of the young."[5]

All the free world will certainly agree on the soundness
of this opinion of Mr. Wallace, although one may find
tremendous difficulty in actually taking measures to effect psychological disarmament in Japan.

Ever since the invasion of Manchuria in 1931, the
Western democracies have hoped that a rise of liberal elements in Japanese politics might effect a change in
Japanese foreign policy. The hope has not been realized.
If it still is cherished after the war, then there should be
a clear understanding that only by means of complete
disarmament under vigilant supervision can the military
clique be removed from control over the country and its
liberal leaders, if any, given the power to guide its national policy in the direction of peaceful development
and cooperation with neighboring states. No doubt there

[4] Hallett Abend, *Pacific Charter*, New York, 1943, pp. 49-50.
[5] *America's Part in World Reconstruction*, by Henry A. Wallace. An
address given on December 28, 1942, the eighty-sixth anniversary of the
birth of Woodrow Wilson, under the auspices of the Woodrow Wilson
Foundation.

will be many difficulties in disarming so chauvinistic a nation as Japan, but those difficulties simply must be faced in view of what is at stake for the world at large as well as for the Pacific region in particular.

Since there are various technical difficulties involved in the actual exercise of control against Japanese rearmament, a considerable body of expert opinion, as shown in the discussions at the Mont Tremblant Conference of the Institute of Pacific Relations, seemed to favor what one conceives as a "realistic" approach to the problem of Japanese disarmament. Some would deem it impracticable as well as impolitic to attempt to keep Japan permanently disarmed. Others would simply rule out as both impossible and unnecessary any plan for continuing long-term discriminatory armament controls against Japan for the simple reason that the victorious powers would soon get tired of enforcing them. In their view, armament control would involve prolonged military occupation of Japan, and that seems to them almost impossible, although they might consider temporary occupation of Tokio by a United Nations force as a symbolic act for bringing home to the Japanese the bitter lesson of their complete defeat. In fact even without discriminatory controls, it is maintained, a defeated Japan with her colonies and her navy presumably lost as a result of the war would actually become unable to rearm without knowledge and in fact collusion on the part of other powers. Thus for a considerable time to come, Japan would not be in a position to endanger peace again in the Far East on a new balance of power.[6]

Without losing sight of such technical and political dif-

[6] Institute of Pacific Relations, *War and Peace in the Pacific,* New York, 1943. A preliminary Report of the Eighth Conference, Mont Tremblant, Quebec, December 4-14, 1942, p. 45, pp. 90-92. See also Peffer, *op. cit.,* pp. 135-6.

ficulties in a prolonged armament control, one should nevertheless recognize that without effective supervision and control against rearming, the so-called disarmament of Japan would be neither permament nor complete. Those experts who think it safe to leave the Japanese after the war to work out the lesson of their own defeat would be guilty of complacency in failing to safeguard against the recurrence of Japanese aggression. Western experts are still apt to underestimate the potentiality of Japan as an aggressive power even with her territory considerably reduced after her defeat. Being a highly industrialized country of over 70,000,000 exceedingly patriotic and virile people most likely imbued with a frenzy of vengeance, Japan would not find much difficulty, in the absence of external control, in rearming herself in order to regain dominant power in the Pacific. The revival of a powerful militaristic Germany in Europe in barely twenty years after her defeat in the First World War should be recalled as a warning against complacency on the part of the United Nations in dealing with the problem of Japanese disarmament.

Moreover, the impracticability of prolonged controls against Japanese rearmament seems to have been unduly exaggerated. In the history of previous wars, it was customary for victorious powers to exercise the right of military occupation, more or less prolonged, for the purpose of enforcing armistice or peace terms. There is no reason why the United Nations should not or could not do likewise in a defeated Japan. Instead of believing, as some do, that "we would not go through with it, any more than we did in Germany," we are entitled to assume that the disastrous consequence of the half-hearted and ineffective control against German rearmament after the last World War should have given Western democracies ample lesson for convincing them of the necessity of enforcing thorough-going control this time against rearming in Japan as well as in other Axis Powers. Such discriminatory controls should be prolonged until a general plan of world disarmament is adopted. It may well be recalled that prolonged controls against Japanese rearmament would be in the long run placed in the charge of an international organization, regional or world-wide, as part of international policing to which the great powers interested in the Pacific region would have anyway to contribute regularly their appropriate share in terms of moral and financial support and of military force.

Territorial Disarmament

Great changes will also have to be made in the territorial limits of Japan. This will be as important as disarmament in reducing Japan's capacity for aggression. In deciding on her new territorial limits, we shall have to take into account both the legitimate claims of interested parties and of the offensive value of the territories in question in Japanese hands.

It goes without saying that Japan must withdraw completely from Manchuria, which automatically would return to Chinese sovereignty. Japan should also be made to relinquish all the territories, both on the continent and scattered across the sea, which she has acquired since 1894 —the year in which her career of conquest started. It does not matter whether such territories shall have been seized during the present war or previously; she should be permitted to retain only those which she had before 1894.[7]

[7] An exception should be made of the Liu-Ch'iu (Ryu Kyu) Islands, between Japan and Formosa. Although Japan annexed them before 1894, they earlier had been tributary to China for 500 years. That, and the fact of the strategic importance of the islands, makes the problem of their disposal a matter for special consideration. At the least the native

The most important of the territories acquired between that date and the outbreak of the Second World War are Korea, Formosa and the Pacific Mandated Islands. The case of Korea will be discussed below. Formosa, a former Chinese province with an almost purely Chinese population, which Japan extorted from China as a condition of peace in 1895, should be restored to China unconditionally. The Mandated Islands, the offensive value of which in Japanese hands has been fully demonstrated, should be placed either under a new mandatory power or under international administration. Unless Soviet Russia desires some other arrangement, the Japanese-controlled southern part of Sakhalin (Karafuto) should be incorporated into the northern part under Soviet sovereignty. Japan should also be required to give up all the territory which she has seized since the outbreak of the present war—parts of mainland China, Hongkong, the Philippines, Hainan, the Netherlands Indies, Indo-China, Malaya, Burma and other areas.

Some writers think so much of Japan's half-century of efficient administration in Formosa and of her economic needs that they would countenance even the continuance of Japanese administration of the island perhaps under an international mandate.[8] Such a view could never be warranted either on moral grounds or by reason of political expediency. Nor would China accept proposals, already advanced by a group of American writers, for internationalization or Anglo-American control of For-

---

people of the islands should be given an opportunity to exercise the right of self-determination. Needless to say, for the purpose of general security, the islands may be used anyway as an air base under international control.

[8] See, for instance, Hugh Byas, *Government by Assassination*, New York, 1942, pp. 359-360.

mosa.[9] China is by no means unmindful of the strategic importance of Formosa as a possible international military base under a general security system. Nevertheless, as a matter of principle, she would insist upon her former territory being returned to her right away and without strings. Should the United Nations wish an international base on the island, as some have proposed, this should be a matter for negotiation with China following the restoration of her territorial sovereignty, not as a condition of it. The Pescadores, another small group of islands off the Chinese coast, ceded to Japan in 1895 along with the Island of Formosa, should also be restored to Chinese sovereignty.[10]

The Japanese Emperor

In this connection, special mention may be made of the controversial problem of the treatment of the Japanese Emperor after the war, in view of the fact that the Emperor is head of Japan's military power as well as the symbol of her national unity, and in view of the precedent in the forced abdication of the German Kaiser after the First World War. Obviously, the United Nations will have to see that the postwar Japanese political regime undergoes such a transformation that no militarist oligarchy can any longer control the state, and that instead some sort of constitutional democratic government shall

[9] See *Fortune*, "Pacific Relations" Supplement, August 1942, pp. 11-12.

[10] People are apt to confuse the Pescadores (*P'eng-hu* in Chinese, and *Bokoto* in Japanese) between China and Formosa with the totally different group, the Liu-Ch'iu Islands, Hallett Abend in *Pacific Charter* gives the following confused description: "Japan was ceded the large and rich semi-tropical island of Formosa and the string of islands once known as the Pescadores and now renamed by Japan the Ryukyu Islands." (p. 54) "The Pescadores completely flank the Chinese coast between the southern tip of Japan proper and the northern tip of Formosa." (p. 55) Here what he describes as the Pescadores are really the Liu-Ch'iu (Ryukyu) Islands.

prevail. Still the question will arise: What should we do about the Emperor? On this point, there is great difference in opinion among writers or experts on the Far East. A radical view would naturally be in favor of forcing Japan to depose the Emperor and establish a republic, after her defeat in the war.[11] On the other hand, some writers advance the conservative opinion that "attempts to force a new and different government or definite constitutional changes on the Japanese people as a condition of peace would not necessarily produce the result desired." Therefore they would not propose to force the abdication of the Emperor or any other constitutional changes in Japan, though they would not stand in the way of the Japanese people if the latter wish themselves to do away with their "eternal, sacred and divine" monarch.[12] Others would in principle abstain from interfering with the strictly internal affairs of Japan. In particular the Imperial House would be considered a valuable institution for postwar Japan in the sense that it could serve as a restraint upon chaotic violence, and the support of a difficult transition to constitutional progress.[13]

In my opinion, the problem at issue is not so simple as to warrant a ready-made solution. No doubt, to interfere with the internal affairs of a defeated enemy, especially concerning a fundamental change in the form of government, is always a very delicate matter which has to be handled with much foresight and tact. Nevertheless, the importance of the Japanese Emperor's position in Japan's state affairs should not be overlooked by the United Nations in formulating a plan for assuring a lasting peace for

[11] See Abend, *op. cit.*, p. 34.

[12] *Fortune, loc. cit.*, p. 14.

[13] *Suggestions for a Far Eastern Peace Settlement,* compiled by M. S. Bates. International Secretariat, Institute of Pacific Relations, New York, May, 1942.

the Pacific region. Up to the present, the Emperor's actual share of responsibility for Japanese military aggression is not clear. Assuming, as we must, that sooner or later there will be set up an international judicial commission to investigate war responsibility and crimes on the part of the Axis civilian and military leaders as well as their rulers including the Japanese Emperor, the fate of the latter may be well left to the commission to determine upon the result of its investigation.[14] Should it be established that the Emperor has been in fact personally responsible along with the militarist clique for the conduct of Japanese aggressive war policy, or even that he has been acting as a willing tool in the hands of the militarists, then there would be sufficient ground for removing the Emperor as a vicious force in Japanese politics which makes for war. On the other hand, if it is proven to the contrary that the Emperor himself has been actually a victim of the Japanese militarists' oligarchy, and that he has tried his best to exercise a moderating or restraining influence upon the aggressive policy ruthlessly pursued by the militarists, both before the outbreak and in the course of the war, that fact would warrant the hope that the Japanese Emperor after the war may lend himself to the support of a peaceful policy to be conducted by liberal elements in politics. In that case, there is no reason why we should not regard the fate of the Emperor after

[14] In fact the Governments of the United States and Great Britain have already announced their agreement upon a proposal to establish a United Nations Commission for the investigation of war crimes to be composed of nationals of the United Nations selected by their governments. As explained by the Lord Chancellor in the House of Lords, on October 7 (1942), the Commission would investigate crimes against nationals of United Nations and the investigation would cover war crimes of offenders irrespective of rank. See *American Journal of International Law*, January, 1943, Editorial Comment on "Retribution of War Crimes," by George Finch.

the war as a purely Japanese internal affair which does not directly affect future international peace, and leave the matter entirely to the discretion of the Japanese people.

The United Nations cannot afford to overlook the fundamental fact that the internal political regime of Japan has had great bearing upon the trends of her external policy. With or without the deposition of the Emperor, Japan must not be allowed to remain under a militaristic regime after the war. Therefore, when we come to the question of the authority in Japan with which the United Nations should deal following her defeat, the answer will be very simple. Under no circumstances should the United Nations treat with the present Tojo Cabinet or any government headed or controlled by military leaders; we should only deal with a government of civilians who are not responsible for Japanese aggression and who can represent the Japanese people. This would have the effect of recognizing and strengthening liberal elements in Japanese politics and helping push Japan's political development in the right direction.

It is noteworthy that some writers of outstanding authority seem very skeptical about the effect of such a discriminatory policy in so far as it is intended to bolster liberal elements in Japan. Some would even hold the extreme view that we should be prepared to make peace with any Japanese government that presents itself, and that "if it is the generals and admirals, so much the better."[15] They deem it impossible to impose upon the Japanese people by coercive methods any political ideology or institution which the United Nations happen to favor; the result, it seems to them, can come about only

15 *War and Peace in the Pacific*, p. 42.

"by inner conviction."[16] In support of their viewpoint they can invoke the authority of the Atlantic Charter whose third point pledges to respect the right "to choose the form of government" to all peoples, presumably including defeated enemy nations such as Japan.

However, there is reasonable ground for the assumption that liberal elements still exist in Japan, and that Japan under a liberal regime stands a better chance of following a policy of peace and cooperation in her international relations. Failing a total social and political upheaval or revolution, as a possible result of her crushing defeat in the war, Japan will be in need of some irresistible external pressure for forcing the militarists out and thus helping the liberal elements rise to power.[17] The most important psychological moment for the United Nations to exercise such pressure on Japan would be the time when the Japanese sue for peace. It may be recalled that President Wilson's decisive stand against Germany's imperial regime in 1918 secured for the German people a fairly advanced democratic parliamentary regime with a moderate foreign policy for nearly fifteen years until Hitler's Nazi party seized power. Should one raise objection to such an interventionist measure on the legal or moral ground that the principle of self-determination has already been enunciated in the Atlantic Charter, attention may be called to the fact that a policy of discriminatory treatment in regard to the political regime of the Axis

[16] Sir George B. Sansom, *Post-War Relations with Japan,* Institute of Pacific Relations, Secretariat Paper, 1942, pp. 11-13. See also Peffer, *op. cit.,* pp. 135-7.

[17] Professor George W. Keeton also envisages the possibility to "encourage and support those elements in Japan's internal life which were previously foremost in welcoming co-operation with western nations and which gave support to Japan's membership of the League of Nations." *Some Factors in a Far Eastern Peace Settlement,* Institute of Pacific Relations, Secretariat Paper, 1942.

powers was also made clear through other equally important official declarations. Thus by the British-Soviet Treaty of Mutual Assistance of May 26, 1942, the two nations undertake not to enter into any negotiation with the Hitlerite Government or any other government in Germany which does not clearly renounce all aggressive intentions. Again, in his address on February 12, 1943, at the White House Correspondents Association dinner, President Roosevelt, referring to the right of the French to have a government of their free choice, declared: "And it will be a free choice in every way. No nation in all the world that is free to make a choice is going to set itself up under a Fascist form of government, or a Nazi form of government, or a Japanese warlord form of government. For such forms are the offspring of seizure of power followed by the abridgement of freedom. Therefore, to these forms of government, Nazism, Fascism and Japanism, if I may coin a new word, the United Nations can properly say two simple words: 'Never again!' For the right of self-determination included in the Atlantic Charter does not carry with it the right of any government anywhere in the world to commit wholesale murder or the right to make slaves of its own people or of any other peoples in the world." In view of such clearly declared discriminatory policy, it is highly doubtful whether the Atlantic Charter could stand in the way of the United Nations putting a ban on a militarist regime in Japan.

In fact this does not necessarily involve deposing the Emperor, revision of the constitution or abolition of what is called "State Shinto," as some draft plans are said to postulate.[18] All that is needed in Japan for the present purpose is just a change of political leadership, a shifting

[18] Sansom, *op. cit.*, p. 11.

of the center of gravity of political power and a reorientation of national policy in relation to other countries.

Reparations

Finally, there is the question of an indemnity which will certainly be raised in the peace settlement with Japan. Here we can only deal with it briefly. Past experience seems to have proved that indemnity or reparation payments are not feasible in the modern world. The United Nations would most likely refrain from imposing any punitive indemnity on the defeated Axis Powers, including Japan. Nevertheless, in the interest of general security as well as on grounds of justice, we have to take the firm stand that for the spoliation Japan has committed and for the devastation, loss of life and property which Japanese aggression has caused to such an unprecedented extent in China, adequate compensation must be exacted. In particular, Japan should be made to surrender in favor of China all her investments, properties and the material assets, no matter whether state owned or belonging to private individuals or corporations, which exist in Manchuria and other parts of Chinese territory. Japan may also be made, as some have suggested, to turn over to China its merchant marine, or at least part of it.[19] As far as is practicable, the transfer of a considerable part of Japanese heavy industries, material and machines to China in aid of her postwar economic reconstruction may also be considered as a reasonable way to compensate for the material damage done China by Japanese aggression.[20] In view of the fact that the Chinese Government has al-

[19] Peffer, *op. cit.*, p. 69.

[20] A similar proposal in regard to the utilization of German industrial plants is as follows: "Let an inter-allied commission dismantle a large percentage of the leading plants in Germany which manufacture airplanes, tractors, chemicals, machine tools, steel, etc., and transport this vital machinery to Poland, Belgium, Holland, France, Greece, Yugoslavia and Russia." As to the practicality of the proposal, one would refer to two

ready had experience in the successful removal in war-time of a considerable part of her industrial machines from the coastal area to the interior and that those plants are in full operation now in Free China to meet war needs, there can be no doubt about the feasibility of removal of Japanese industrial plants to be set in operation on Chinese soil after the war.

The disarmament of Japan and other matters discussed above are intended not purely for the sake of just retribution but mainly as a deterrent to future aggression. The United Nations could not countenance a policy of keeping Japan down forever or "bleeding the Japanese white." On the contrary, both on grounds of justice and in the interest of general peace and security, it will be necessary, as many far-seeing persons have asserted, to readjust allied postwar policy so as to enable a reformed Japan "to live and prosper,"[21] as well as to encourage her to collaborate in a new international order which the United Nations wish to promote.[22] Japan could equally benefit from the Atlantic Charter both in its general assurance of freedom from fear and want, and in respect of its special promise of equal access to the trade and the raw materials of the world which are needed for her economic prosperity.

---

known facts; "one, the removal by the Russians of a good part of their industrial equipment from the west to points beyond the Urals. This was done so successfully that Russia has been able to equip huge armies with superior equipment for her present counter-offensives. Two, the purchase by Chile of copper and steel plants as quoted in a news dispatch from Santiago in the *New York Times* under date of February 7. These plants were expected to be in operation in Chile before the end of 1943. There seems to be no doubt that the machinery of huge plants can be quickly and economically moved to foreign countries." (Lawrence Fertig's letter to the *New York Times*, March 9, 1943). The same observation can be made on the transfer of Japanese industrial plants to China.

[21] In particular, Professor Peffer takes a very "realistic" view in this matter. *Op. cit.*, Chapter 7, "Japan's Legitimate Needs."

[22] Sansom, *op. cit.*, p. 15.

CHAPTER III

READJUSTMENT OF CHINA'S RELATIONS WITH OTHER POWERS

Abolition of the Unequal Treaties

The abrogation of unequal treaties, now at last practically achieved, has been one of the outstanding diplomatic issues between China and the Great Powers ever since the Chinese nationalist revolution began. By means of these treaties as well as through other forms of political influence the foreign Powers acquired extraterritorial rights and special privileges of various kinds which have been seriously detrimental to China's sovereignty and national welfare. It is no exaggeration to say that in agitating for the abolition of the unequal treaties China has been seeking to achieve international harmony and justice as well as national freedom. Many farsighted westerners have recognized the desirability of a fundamental change in their countries' treaty relations with China. Germany and Austria lost their extraterritorial rights in the first world war and Russia relinquished hers voluntarily after the 1917 Revolution; unfortunately, the other foreign Powers were slow to relinquish the privileged positions which they continued to enjoy for almost a century.

The supreme effort towards abolishing the unequal treaties was begun by China almost immediately following the establishment of the National Government in Nanking in 1927. China's foreign policy in that period aimed, above all, to gain tariff autonomy, and to abolish extraterritorial rights enjoyed by foreign powers. The United States Government led the way to recognize China's tariff autonomy by the Sino-American agreement of July 25, 1928, signed at Peking. Other Treaty Powers followed suit. By the spring of 1930, Japan was the only power that had not agreed to China's claim for tariff autonomy. With the conclusion, after much difficulty, of a Sino-Japanese tariff agreement, on May 26, 1930, China's national aspiration in the matter of tariff was finally realized.

On the other hand, up to 1931 no substantial result was gained by China in her negotiations for the relinquishment of extraterritorial rights. Five Treaty Powers, namely, Belgium, Italy, Portugal, Denmark and Spain did consent to relinquish their extraterritorial rights in China by the respective new treaties they signed with the Chinese National Government during the year 1928. But even these treaties were rendered inoperative by the fact that many other powers, especially Great Britain, the United States and France still failed to reach an agreement with China on the relinquishment of their similar privileges in China.

China's persistent effort to terminate the unequal treaties was, however, brought to an abrupt end by the Japanese invasion of Manchuria following the Mukden Incident of September 18, 1931. The National Government found itself so deeply absorbed in the grave new crisis that it had to put off for the time being further action for abolishing the treaties and the whole matter was left in suspense. Indeed it was noteworthy that for a considerable time the extraterritorial rights and other privileges were being used, though often with great difficulty, by those foreign Powers still enjoying them as a bulwark in the defense of their position in China against the demands of the Japanese invaders.

The Second World War has simplified this problem. Not even the staunchest die-hards expect to see the old order restored in China's foreign relations, no matter what the outcome of the war. Indeed, Great Britain and the United States have already announced relinquishment of their extraterritorial rights in China. It goes without saying that the special rights or interests claimed by Japan or imposed upon China by that country should also be wiped out. In the postwar relations between China and foreign Powers, the principles of equality and reciprocity should be followed in concluding treaties as well as in all other transactions. All extraterritorial rights should be abolished. There should be no more foreign consular jurisdictions and no more foreign concessions or settlements in China. All the leased territories should be returned unconditionally to Chinese jurisdiction. Foreign nations should no longer be permitted to station troops or gunboats within Chinese territory.

Only by such a fundamental readjustment of her relations with foreign Powers could China really be freed from foreign domination and set firmly on the course of political and economic progress. At the same time the development of a normal, free relationship between China and the nations of the West would help create a more friendly atmosphere for international cooperation.

As a matter of fact, recent events raise the hope that these objectives may be achieved even before the war is ended. A decisive step to that effect was taken by the American Government on October 9, 1942, the eve of the Chinese Republic Anniversary, when it notified the Chinese Government that it was prepared in concert with the British Government, to relinquish its extraterritorial and related rights in China. This announcement was soon followed on October 24 by the submission to China by the American Government of a draft treaty designed to accomplish the immediate relinquishment of American extraterritorial rights. The draft treaty was presumed to be of such a wide and comprehensive scope that it could cover the entire system of foreign rights or privileges.

Sino-American negotiations on the basis of the American draft resulted in the signing of a new treaty at Washington on January 11, 1943, relinquishing American extraterritorial rights in China. A similar treaty between China and Great Britain was signed on the same date in Chungking. With the conclusion of these new treaties ended the privileged position enjoyed in China by Britain and the United States under the so-called unequal treaties for almost a century. The new treaties put an end to their extraterritorial rights and consular jurisdiction within China, the special rights enjoyed by them in the so-called treaty ports especially in the form of settlement or concession, in the diplomatic quarter at Peking (Peiping), and in the International Settlements at Shanghai and Amoy including special courts at Shanghai and Amoy for the trial of their respective nationals. Great Britain and the United States also gave up their rights under the Peking Protocol signed in 1901 after the Boxer War, including the right to station troops on Chinese territory, and the special rights enjoyed heretofore by Britain and American naval vessels in Chinese waters as well as their special rights in regard to coasting trade and inland navigation in the waters of China.

With the conclusion of the new Sino-American and Sino-British treaties, a new chapter has opened in China's foreign relations. The fact that a four-day holiday was decreed by the Chinese Government to celebrate the occasion is a fair indication of the extent to which China stresses the importance of the new treaties as a decisive step towards achieving her national aspiration for equality and freedom. The statement made by Generalissimo Chiang Kai-shek following the signing of the treaties is even more significant in so far as it represents Chinese sentiment in appreciating the timely action of the United States and Great Britain. In the statement given to the armies and people of China, the Generalissimo declared: "Today marks a new epoch in China's history and today Britain and America have lighted a light to guide Man's progress on the road to equality and freedom for all peoples."[1]

In order to complete the process of abolishing the unequal treaties, at least two steps still remain to be taken. First, the existence of leased territories on Chinese soil has been one of the most noxious features of China's foreign relations. Yet the problem is not touched upon in the new Sino-British Treaty as far as the leased territory of Kowloon is concerned.[2] It is by no means unreasonable to hope that an early settlement of the issue of leased territory may be effected in some appropriate way.[3] Second, there still remain some Treaty Powers which legally enjoy extraterritorial rights in China. These powers should

[1] *Voice of China*, Chinese News Service, New York, January 13, 1943. For the full texts of the two treaties, see *China at War*, Chinese News Service, New York, March, 1943.

[2] The British Government was said to have declined to discuss the question of Kowloon in its negotiations with China for the relinquishment of extraterritorial rights, probably for the reason that the Peninsula of Kowloon has been considered an integral part of Hongkong from an economic as well as a military point of view. But how could Great Britain expect to retain control of Hongkong after the war? This question is further treated below (pp. 85-7).

[3] As a result of Japanese forces moving into the leased territory of Kwangchow-wan, the French lease on that territory has been unilaterally terminated by China through a formal denunciation of the convention of 1899 which gave France a lease for a period of 99 years.

be approached as soon as possible for a similar agreement
to relinquish such rights.

Treatment of Chinese Abroad

Between China and some of the Western Powers there
is another long-standing issue which constantly consti-
tutes a serious cause of friction in international relations
as well as of unnecessary racial antagonism, and therefore
must be equitably settled as soon as possible. It concerns
the treatment of Chinese abroad. It is well known that
Chinese have long been subject to various harsh and unjust measures of restriction or exclusion in many foreign
countries around the Pacific—in Southeast Asia, in the
British Dominions, in the South American countries as
well as in the United States. Whatever motive these
countries might have had for such measures against Chinese
in the past, this kind of outrageous racial discrimination
should no longer be tolerated in a free world after the
war. Indeed the issue is already being raised through
public discussion, and no statesman with vision can afford
to ignore it. As the United States was almost the first to
adopt an exclusion law against Chinese, it should be expected now to lead the way to such a change of policy as
to free Chinese from any discriminatory treatment in
either immigration or naturalization. Needless to say,
China does not expect the United States or any other
nation to go so far as to admit unlimited Chinese immigrants. What the Chinese ask for is to be treated,
wherever they go, on an equal footing with other civilized
peoples, without being subject to legal discrimination on
account of racial or national distinction.

As far as the Chinese problem in the United States
is concerned, the issue has been reduced to just a revision
of law so as to make Chinese eligible for citizenship and

place Chinese immigrants on the same quota basis as most other nations. In the legal aspect, Mr. T. C. Shen has well pointed out, there are two laws of the United States which deprive Chinese of the right to become American citizens, namely the Naturalization Law and the Chinese Exclusion Law. The former applies to Chinese as well as some other Asiatics, and the latter to Chinese only. As the American Naturalization Law of 1790, revised in 1870, provided that "any alien being a free white person may be admitted to become a citizen" of the United States, a native of China, of the Mongolian race, has long since been considered not a white person within the meaning of the term of the Naturalization Law, and therefore not entitled to become a citizen of the United States. Specifically, the Chinese Exclusion Act of 1882 prohibited all United States courts from admitting Chinese to citizenship. As regards immigration, Chinese are subject to double exclusion, i.e., under the Chinese Exclusion Law as well as under the general Immigration Act of 1924 which excludes "aliens ineligible to citizenship" from the quota system. In Mr. Shen's opinion, "the Chinese labor question is now dead. Most of the provisions of the Chinese exclusion laws have been either superseded or incorporated by the more stringent and more comprehensive immigration laws. Except for a few provisions, such as 'section 6 certificate' and 'port of entry,' the so-called Chinese exclusion laws have practically become nullified. Therefore the repeal of Chinese exclusion laws would not change the situation materially. The only important issue now between China and the United States is the non-naturalization of Chinese. If the American laws were amended so as to admit a negligible number of Chinese on the same quota basis as Caucasians and allow them to be eligible for naturalization, all Chinese exclusion questions would be satisfactorily settled."[4]

If the United States Congress could take the necessary legislative measures for removing all legal discrimination against Chinese in matters of immigration and naturalization, that would be adequate to meet the desired end. Otherwise, a new treaty or a clause in a new treaty concluded between China and the United States specifically making Chinese eligible for naturalization and placing Chinese immigration on a quota basis would accomplish the same purpose without the necessity of seeking legislative measures on the part of Congress, since a treaty made by the United States Government is the supreme law of the land and supersedes any precedent legislative act to the contrary.

Apparently most of the writers on the subject favor the quota system as a more practicable way to settle the Chinese immigration issue in America, although proposals in favor of other solutions have also been put forth. For instance, the editors of *Fortune* have suggested that the American Government "should conclude at once an immigration and naturalization treaty with China, providing for the reciprocal admission of certain classes, such as merchants and intellectuals, and making eligible for naturalization all those admitted to permanent residence." Chinese "unskilled labor" could, in their opinion, be barred without offense if the principle of equality is admitted by barring American unskilled labor from China.[5] But one has to realize that class discrimination is too delicate a matter to be specifically embodied in a treaty, and control of emigration may be better left to the discre-

---

[4] T. C. Shen, *What Chinese Exclusion Really Means*, China Institute in America, New York, 1942.
    [5] *Fortune, loc. cit.*, p. 28.

tion of Chinese home authorities as an administrative measure. On the whole, it seems that the quota system will be in the present circumstances a more simple and practicable solution for the Chinese exclusion issue between China and the United States.[6]

In order to appreciate China's consistent stand on this issue, one needs only to recall that the first Chinese nation-wide boycott was directed against American goods in 1905 when the controversy over the Chinese exclusion issue between China and America reached a climax; also that at the Paris Peace Conference in 1919, the Chinese Delegation, despite its opposition to the Japanese in all other respects, actually chose to support the Japanese demand for insertion in the then proposed Covenant of the League of Nations a clause establishing "the principle of equality of nations and just treatment of their nationals." Now that the Chinese are fighting side by side with the United States in a common war for freedom, it is not unreasonable to expect that the American nation should seize this psychological moment to effect a settlement of the whole issue in order to redress a long-standing grievance on the part of China and demonstrate American friendship and respect for the Chinese nation. A friendly gesture like this would not fail to have an inestimable moral effect upon the Chinese people and to brighten their outlook both in the prosecution of the common war and in postwar relations with America. Indeed, the whole matter would have been much simplified had the Chinese immigration issue been settled at one and the same time with the

---

[6] According to Mr. T. C. Shen, on the quota basis, "the annual quota for Chinese would only be 87. Since the minimum quota is 100, the nominal quota allowed to Chinese is 100." The total number of Chinese abroad was estimated in 1936 to be about 7,838,900 persons, of which only about 75,000, as officially estimated, live in the United States. See *Statesman's Year-Book,* 1941, p. 774; Abend, *op. cit.,* p. 74; *Chinese Year-Book,* 1940-1941, pp. 103-105.

relinquishment of America's extraterritorial rights in China by the treaty recently concluded between the two countries. However, there are signs that enlightened public opinion in the United States begins to sense the importance of an early settlement of the Chinese exclusion issue in the midst of the war. A bill "to grant to the Chinese rights of entry to the United States and rights to citizenship" was actually introduced in Congress in February, 1943 by Representative Martin J. Kennedy of New York. The bill specifically calls for the repeal of what is known as the "Chinese Exclusion Act" together with amendment of the statute which denies Chinese, along with other Asiatics, the right of naturalization no matter how long they reside in the United States. Representative Kennedy, in a letter to Mme. Chiang Kai-shek, spoke of the Exclusion Act as being enacted without justification when "the importation of cheap Chinese labor brought with it a wave of alarmed misunderstanding and prejudice on the part of some of our people."[7]

Besides the Kennedy bill several other bills were introduced in Congress with a more or less similar object in view. This fact certainly indicates how far the question of settling the Chinese exclusion issue has now become, as never before, a matter of practical politics in the United States. In fact, public hearings have already been held in the House Immigration Committee before which many prominent citizens of various classes have testified to the injustice of the existent legal discriminations against Chinese and the need of their repeal. Although the Committee has thus far failed to report out any of the bills in favor of repealing the Chinese exclusion acts, the issue is still being kept alive in Congress. After a setback recently in

[7] See *New York Times*, February 20, 1943; *Voice of China*, February 27, 1943.

the House Immigration Committee, sponsors of a movement to repeal Chinese exclusion acts immediately offered a new bill which was introduced by Representative Gosset of Texas in the House. The new bill, as reported in the *New York Herald Tribune* (June 8, 1943), would provide: (1) a quota of slightly more than 100 annually for Chinese immigration to the United States; (2) naturalization of Chinese as citizens of the United States; (3) division of the quota allowed Chinese, permitting 75 per cent of it to be allotted Chinese residents of China proper and the remainder to Chinese residing outside China, in order to prevent immigration of Chinese under quotas of other countries. New hearings, possibly including testimony by State Department representatives, would be held. It was hoped that the Committee would be able this time to report to the House a measure which could be acted upon before Congress recessed for the summer. Failure or undue delay in passing such a measure as to accord Chinese equal treatment in matters of immigration and naturalization would evidently create great disappointment and serious misunderstanding in China to the detriment of friendly relationship of the two great allied nations. In this matter American political leaders, let us hope, will not fall behind public opinion but, on the contrary, lead it in seeking immediately an equitable settlement of the issue.

CHAPTER IV

RACIAL AND NATIONAL PROBLEMS OF THE PACIFIC REGION

Not less important—though certainly more delicate—are the issues raised by the great variety of races and nations which exist in the Pacific region. Most of them are related to the problem of the future status of colonies or possessions heretofore ruled by the Great Powers. It is of paramount concern to the Pacific countries that these issues should be settled in a just and practical manner. The Japanese slogan of "Asia for the Asiatics" is no doubt pure political propaganda and will be dismissed as such by most intelligent Asiatics. Many and various racial and national problems do exist, nevertheless, and the hope of building up a lasting peace in the Pacific depends to a large extent on their correct solution. Almost all the subject peoples and colonies in this region, with the sole exception of the Philippines which have secured a definite promise of independence by 1946, have age-old grievances against their rulers. Those of them who are politically mature cherish aspirations for political or national freedom and have actually been striving for its realization. Since the United Nations are committed to an all-out fight for world freedom, it would be both illogical and impolitic, from either the long-term or the short-term view, for them not to help realize such legitimate aspirations.

36

India

The most urgent case is that of India. Her population of 390 to 400 millions is the second largest in the world, and she has all the characteristics of a distinct civilization. Today she has become one of the most important factors in world politics. In the right circumstances, the people of India could play a major role both in the present fight for world freedom and in the shaping of a postwar order in the Pacific. For the sake of freedom and peace, farsighted and fair-minded persons everywhere want to see India's national aspirations fully realized after the war. Generalissimo Chiang Kai-shek was simply voicing the general sentiment of the free world when, after a series of conferences with India leaders, he urged the British to give India real political power, declaring: "I sincerely hope and confidently believe that Britain, without waiting for any demand on the part of the people of India, will, as speedily as possible, give them real political power so that they may be in a position to further develop their spiritual and material strength, and thus realize that their participation in the war is not merely aid to the anti-aggression nations for victory, but also the turning point in their struggle for India's freedom."

Lord Cranborne, then British Colonial Secretary, stated on February 24, 1942, that the British Government was "in favor of India's political freedom," although he qualified this by adding that "if the Indian leaders would get together and devise some scheme which would be satisfactory to all, the Indian problem would be satisfactorily solved." Prime Minister Churchill's announcement of a definite British offer of Dominion status and Sir Stafford Cripps' subsequent mission raised hopes of an early realization of Indian aspirations. Although the

Cripps Mission failed to achieve its immediate objective, due to the rejection of the British proposals by all the Indian political parties, it marked a real turning point in Indian affairs.

From a long-range view, one can be confident that, whatever disturbances or other unhappy events have happened and may still happen in India during the war because of the serious disagreement between the British Government and the Indian National Congress Party as to the proper way of realizing India's political freedom, there is no question about eventually achieving that supreme objective after the war. Then, the pressure of British enlightened public opinion as well as world opinion should be strong enough to compel British states-men to move rapidly towards settlement of the Indian problem to the good of all parties concerned. It would be too delicate a matter for outsiders to "dictate" any definite measure to Great Britain for adoption in her actual rule over India. Yet it seems a reasonable sug-gestion, favored by a number of writers, that under the present circumstances, just for the sake of British-Indian unity in the war effort, the British Government might well, apart from making necessary readjustments in war-time government for securing maximum cooperation on the part of Indian leaders in the defense of India, pro-ceed immediately by a solemn declaration to set a definite time for India's complete freedom.[1] In this respect, a precedent can be found in the American procedure of assuring the date of Philippine independence by the Act of 1934.

It is to be added that far-seeing people from other countries, without taking sides with one political group

[1] See Anne O'Hare McCormick's article in the *New York Times,* "A Discoverer of the New World in the East," (Oct. 28, 1942); and Alvin Johnson's letter to the Editor (*New York Times,* Nov. 8, 1942).

as against others in India, are all concerned with seeing that the war effort of the United Nations is not further impeded by continuance of the political deadlock in India. One proposal from an important Indian source for breaking this deadlock seems to be equally worth considering. The essential point of this proposal is first of all to Indianize the present Government of India by replacing the three remaining British members of the Viceroy's Executive Council by Indians. This would be an important first step towards peaceful transfer of governmental power into the hands of Indian leaders. Actually some sort of political *modus vivendi* is needed in India not only for the purpose of tiding over the crisis for the period of war but also with a view to preparing the ground for the political reconstruction of India after the war.[2]

Korea

The case of Korea is perhaps the simplest. Korea was forcibly and fraudulently annexed by Japan in 1910, and the Korean people have never ceased to show their opposition to Japanese rule. Increasing numbers of Koreans have been fighting or working in China against the common enemy. There is no reason why this once independent kingdom, with a population of 22 million and a civilization more ancient than that of the Japanese, should not be given political freedom after the defeat of Japan. It is fitting that a representative of China, Dr. Hu Shih, should have been the first man in public life to remind the world of Korea's claim for freedom by

[2] For this purpose, a second step was actually proposed involving the setting up of an Exploratory Commission which would include Indian leaders representing the points of view of the various political parties. See Frederick V. Field, "The Mont Tremblant Conference," *Far Eastern Survey*, January 11, 1943; also War and Peace in the Pacific, p. 65.

saying that at the coming peace conference "the wishes of the 22 million people in Korea should be given a fair hearing and just consideration and steps should be taken to see sovereign rights and self-government restored to these people." President Roosevelt has also specifically mentioned "the people of Korea" as one of those whose future freedom depends upon a victory of the United Nations.

It would be superfluous to dwell further on the case of Korea's freedom, were it not for the fact that there are still writers of authority who would for various reasons let Japan retain control of Korea even after the war is won.[3] In order to further clarify the issue, a number of major facts may well be recalled.

In the first place, Korea, being only a little more than one hundred miles from Japan, is a natural bridge between the Asia mainland and the Japanese islands. This peninsula has been serving as the main strategic base for the Japanese advance into the interior of the Asiatic continent under the impetus of the so-called "continental policy." In the interest of future peace and security, the Japanese must be ejected completely from the Korean peninsula so that Japan would no longer retain a foothold on the mainland enabling her to resume continental expansion.

Second, historically, ever since the latter part of the last century, the fate of Korea has been one of the great disturbing factors in Far Eastern politics. At least two major wars were fought on the issue of Korea in the past forty years. In 1894 Japan made war on China in dispute for supremacy over the Kingdom of Korea. Again, the Russo-Japanese War in 1904-5 was an armed contest just as much for control of the Korean peninsula

[3] See Byas, *op. cit.*, pp. 359-60.

as for the domination of Manchuria. As a nation, the Koreans have never given up the idea of fighting the Japanese in order to restore their freedom whenever there is a chance to do so. In default of a satisfactory settlement of the Korean question after the war, it is most likely that Korea will remain a storm center in the Far East because of international rivalry as well as national agitation.

Third, before falling into the Japanese control, Korea was a separate kingdom which, although nominally under Chinese suzerainty, had treaty relations with major Western Powers. Moreover, after the Sino-Japanese War, Korea's independence was solemnly proclaimed by the Sino-Japanese Peace Treaty of 1895, and further recognized later in the Anglo-Japanese Treaty of Alliance as first concluded in 1902. Thus the independent status of Korea was embodied in international agreements; maintenance of its independence and territorial integrity thus became a matter of international concern. Yet when Japan proceeded first to set a protectorate over Korea in 1905 and then to proclaim formal annexation of the kingdom in 1910, not even a formal protest was made against these outrageous acts, to say nothing of a declaration of non-recognition, by the Western Treaty Powers. Indeed, both the United States and Great Britain were suspected of acquiescing in the whole shameful transaction. Anyway it was the British and American benevolent attitude towards Japanese annexationist designs that contributed to stabilizing Japan's hold on Korea, thus paving the way for her continental expansion. Would it be too much to expect that Great Britain and the United States, now the two leading Powers of the United Nations, will not repeat that mistaken policy of the past, but instead will at once right a wrong done to the Korean people by seeking to free their country completely from Japan's yoke at the end of the war? This is obviously a matter not only of justice but of political expediency as well.

Finally, if it should appear that the Korean people, after liberation from the Japanese yoke, still need friendly advice and assistance in the initial stages of their political freedom, the United States would be in the best position to assume this responsibility. This is true not only because of American disinterestedness and the traditional friendship between the United States and Korea, but also because American financial resources would be needed to help the newly freed country in its effort to rebuild a national life. It may be objected that the United States would be reluctant to assume a mandate over Korea. A few obvious reasons can be advanced for this view. One is that to exercise a mandate over a far away country would be a difficult assignment technically for the United States. Another and more important reason is that this would be regarded by the American public opinion as an extremely retrogressive step: it would look like parcelling out colonies among the victors—"straight imperialism." In principle, it may be added, independence for Korea would be the only course consistent with the war aims of the United Nations, apparently as indicated in the Atlantic Charter. As a matter of fact, the United States was once offered a mandate over Armenia after the First World War and that offer was declined.

However, any arrangement for assistance to Korea after the war, whether in the form of a mandatory regime or otherwise, should be worked out on the basis of international guarantees as well as under international supervision. Moreover the responsibility America would assume in rendering assistance, as suggested above, to Korea need not necessarily put the United States in the position of a mandatory power in the full sense nor would it necessarily be inconsistent with the independence of a Korean republic. In fact postwar aid in rebuilding the national life of a restored Korea will vary in character in different stages of her political development. After the Japanese are driven out of Korea, the country may be under military occupation by the United Nations which will have to assume the responsibility of insuring security, order and welfare of the Korean people as an emergency measure for a period. In this stage the question of the need of any power or combination of powers rendering assistance to Korea will not arise. This question will only arise when the armistice period comes to an end and the Koreans begin to undertake the government of their own country. At that time the problem of foreign aid will have to be dealt with separately in its different aspects. As far as military assistance is concerned, it will be a matter of international responsibility; on account of her vulnerable geographical position and small national resources, Korea could hardly expect to be self-sufficing in national defense. The security of the new Korea will depend anyway upon the existence of a system of collective security, regional or world-wide. Perhaps the Korean peninsula may be well chosen as a strategic base on the Asia mainland for stationing an international force under the collective security plan, which naturally would help strengthen the defense of that country. At any rate it does not seem likely that any power which undertakes to render assistance to an independent Korea would be called upon to assume special military responsibility for her defense apart from its regular share in sustaining the collective security system.

There remain only three kinds of aid which would be required for Korea during a transition period. One is political advice. This may not involve actual responsibility in the conduct of the Korean government which the Koreans will probably be left to organize and operate by themselves after the United Nations military regime is withdrawn. But the fact that a powerful and disinterested nation like America is placed in a position to extend friendly advice to Korea would be sure to have the most helpful moral effect on the political development as well as the international relations of the newly freed nation. Yet America can help the Korean people most of all by rendering advice and assistance in the administrative and economic fields. American aid in these fields will be a less difficult or delicate task from the American viewpoint, but a more substantial contribution towards rebuilding Korean national life.

Thus when we look more fully into the different aspects of the Korean problem, there is nothing particularly difficult or impossible or repulsive to the American mind in the suggestion that the United States be given the responsibility of rendering assistance to a restored Korea in a transition period. Assuming that the United States will continue to sustain a policy of international cooperation after the war in the interest of general peace, there is no reason why the American Government should not be ready to render assistance to Korea as the common interest of the United Nations requires. Should the United States be in a position to tender political advice to a reborn Korea and to provide her government with the service of experienced administrators and technical experts as well as with financial assistance, it would certainly be an invaluable contribution towards rebuilding Korea's national life as well as a great help in the initial exercise of her newly restored freedom.[4]

It is to be admitted that many well-informed writers, with full sympathy for the cause of Korea, have expressed doubt about "the capacity of the Korean people to sustain full immediate autonomy," especially in view of the fact that they have been under Japanese enslavement for nearly forty years. There is also substantial agreement even among ardent advocates of Korea's independence that some sort of interim arrangement for outside assistance to the newly-freed people will be inevitable before they may be safely left alone to work out their own salvation.[5]

Various suggestions have already been put forward in respect of the future government of Korea. Apart from the idea advanced by some that Japan should, under supervision, be entrusted with the mandatory role in respect of Korea, which must be simply ruled out as absurdly unjust as well as obviously unworkable, there are at least two important suggestions which might receive serious attention. One is a Sino-Russian joint control in Korea; the other is international administration of Korea.[6] Although there is much to be said for these ideas, neither of them could be worked out without involving serious political complications as well as technical difficulties. On the whole, one must admit that American assistance, in whatever form, under international supervision would be a much simpler and safer scheme to carry

[4] It is interesting to note that an American authority has expressed the view that "probably the United States would do a good deal for Korea." Tyler Dennett, *Security in the Pacific and the Far East*. American Council, Institute of Pacific Relations, 1942, p. 28.

[5] See Sir George Sansom, *Postwar Relations with Japan*. Secretariat, Institute of Pacific Relations, 1942, p. 3; George W. Keeton, *Some Factors in a Far Eastern Peace Settlement*. Secretariat, Institute of Pacific Relations, 1942, pp. 17-19; Abend, *op. cit.*, Chapter VI.

[6] See *Fortune, loc. cit.*, p. 30; Peffer, *op. cit.*, p. 68.

out both for the good of the Korean nation and in the interest of world peace.

Dependencies of Western Powers

The postwar fate of Indo-China cannot be settled yet. But one thing should be made clear: the conditions which existed in that country under French rule should not be restored after the Japanese have withdrawn. Good government, at least, should be guaranteed to the native people, and they should be given a fair chance to prepare themselves for self-government. Other subject peoples in the Pacific area, such as those of Malaya, Burma and the Netherlands Indies, come in a different category. But their interests should be given fair consideration in the postwar reconstruction. It must be recognized that the goal for these people is self-government to be attained by progressive stages.

A few guiding ideas for the solution of these colonial problems may be submitted. The ultimate status of most of the large dependencies might be either complete political independence or full self-government in the form of Dominion status or home rule. At the same time, one must admit that, with the exception of India, hardly any of them has reached a stage of political maturity which would ensure a successful exercise of immediate freedom. It is pretty well agreed that the subject peoples of the Pacific region should not be returned to the position they occupied before the war. Yet it would be premature and even dangerous to leave them to themselves immediately after the war in a region where international relations as well as racial problems are so complicated. To do this might create chaos instead of order.[7]

[7] For general information on political conditions of these dependencies before Japanese invasion, see Emerson, Mills and Thompson, *Government and Nationalism in Southeast Asia*, I.P.R., New York, 1942; *The*

There should be a period of tutelage, then, during which the native people would have an opportunity to prepare themselves for self-government. The best way to promote this would be to give the natives more education, to hasten their economic emancipation, and to allow them to acquire political training by participating more and more in local administration. In the meantime, each colonial government, whether in charge of an international commission or under a colonial or mandatory Power, should adjust its educational, financial and administrative systems to serve the best interests of the natives. The policy which was so successfully pursued by the United States in the Philippines should be followed as far as practicable as a model for colonial administration in the whole Pacific area.

To put it in President Roosevelt's own words, "the history of the Philippine Islands in the last forty-four years provides in a very real sense a pattern for the future of other small nations and peoples of the world." But "such a pattern is based on two important factors. The first is that there shall be a period of preparation, through the dissemination of education and the recognition of physical, social and economic needs. The second is that there be a period of training for ultimate independent sovereignty, through the practice of more and more self-government, beginning with the local government, and passing on through the various steps to complete statehood."[8] Now that the postwar independence of the Philippines is assured, there is no reason why equally successful

---

Annals, American Academy of Political and Social Science, March, 1943— "Southeastern Asia and the Philippines," especially the article "Some Problems of Postwar Reconstruction," by Professor Lennox A. Mills.

[8] President Roosevelt's address commemorating the 7th Anniversary of the Philippines Commonwealth Government (*New York Times,* Nov. 16, 1942).

attainment of nationhood could not be secured for other native peoples through the same process of progressive and enlightened tutelage.

It is impossible to stipulate a uniform system of administration for all the colonies and dependencies in question. Different regimes would have to be used in different circumstances. Some writers have advocated a federation or grouping to be called the "Indonesian Union," composed of British Malaya, the Netherlands Indies, the Philippines, Burma, and, later on, Thailand and Indo-China.[9] Others would create an Indonesian State or establish a "South China Sea Area" as a separate state, to be composed of Thailand, British Malaya, all the British and Dutch islands in Indonesia, and Portuguese Timor.[10] The idea of binding such heterogeneous human groups and geographical units into a federation must be ruled out as impracticable. The people of these countries do not have enough common interests and mutual understanding to support a federal union, nor have they sufficient political experience to operate one. Whatever the scheme is called, federation, union, or state, in practice, it would be government through an international commission exercising its rule over a vast area. Such international regime would hardly work, in view of the serious conflicts of interests and policies which might arise among the Powers forming it.

Thailand

One of the most objectionable features of the *Fortune* scheme for an Indonesian or South China Sea Area State is its presumption of the destruction of Thailand as an independent state after the war. Whatever economic and

[9] See Corbett, *Post-war Worlds,* I.P.R., New York, 1942, pp. 73-80.
[10] *Fortune, loc. cit.,* pp. 6-7. See also Raymond Kennedy, *The Ageless Indies,* New York, 1942.

military reasons one may advance for attaching Thailand
to a large geographical grouping, such cold-blooded destruction of the very Siamese state simply to suit some
political purpose, even of an international nature, would
be an intolerable and outrageous measure, smacking too
much of Hitler's methods to be attempted by the United
Nations. One need only to be reminded that actually,
besides China and Japan, Thailand is the only independent state in the Far East. How could it be a consistent
policy for the United Nations to conceive of a scheme involving destruction of a state long in existence while we
profess to stand for freedom of subject peoples in Asia
with the view of making new national states in the near
future?

One claim is that "Thai independence has always been
more formal than real. During the twenties it survived
precariously, protected by rivalry between the British and
the French; each intent on keeping the other out of
what was not really a national state but a strategic area."[11]
This seems rather unconvincing in so far as it is to justify
destruction of the Thai state. It is true that the Siamese
State has had hard times in trying to maintain its independence because of its precarious position between two
great colonial Powers. But this is also true of other
small countries in a similar position, such as Persia in
Asia and Belgium in Europe and could never justify destruction of a nation's independence, however nominal it
might be. Another important reason given for destruction
of Thailand as an independent state is that this solution
would "relieve Thailand of the possibility of Chinese control, now favored in China."[12] To destroy a state in order

[11] *Fortune, loc. cit.,* p. 7.
[12] *Fortune* editors' reply to the Thai minister's protests, *Fortune,* Oct.
1942, p. 9.

to save it from possible control by another country is certainly a clumsy solution. As a matter of fact, however, neither government leaders nor the general public in China have ever shown any political designs on Thailand.[13] There is absolutely no ground for the allegation that Chinese control of Thailand is "now favored in China." On the contrary, official statements recently reported from Chungking have shown sympathy for the Thai people under Japanese enslavement, and have looked forward to a restoration of Thailand's independence after the war is won by the United Nations. In a message to the armed forces and people of Thailand on February 26, 1943, Generalissimo Chiang Kai-shek gave his solemn word that "China, as well as her allies, have no territorial ambitions in Thailand and harbor no intentions of undermining her sovereignty and independence. This will continue to be true in the future as it has been in the past. The Thais, however, should recognize the fact that their territory is now practically under Japanese occupation, their people enslaved and their sovereignty and independence violated by the Japanese, while the territory and freedom of Thailand can only be restored to her through the victory of China and her allies."[14]

Of course, China has had a good many grievances against Thailand; in particular, the Thai Government has oppressed the Chinese in that country, and it has entered the war on the side of Japan. Nevertheless, though that would give China a special interest in the treatment

[13] The only exceptional case is, as recently reported by a news dispatch, that a certain daily paper in Chungking advocated China's rule over Thailand after the war. But so far that report has not been confirmed and even if a Chungking paper did express such an extreme view, this isolated case would by no means reflect Chinese public opinion in general.

[14] *Voice of China*, February 27, 1943.

of Thailand when victory is won, it should not serve as a reason for destroying Thai independence. Undoubtedly, after the war Thailand would be expected to effect such adjustments both in domestic policy and in international relations as to insure good relations and better economic cooperation with neighboring countries. In particular, it might perhaps be subjected to complete disarmament as a peace condition.

Colonial Trusteeship

As a matter of fact, responsibility for the administration of the large colonies and dependencies will probably be resumed after the war by the original ruling Powers, which will certainly try hard to regain hold of their possessions. In his speech at the Lord Mayor's dinner at the Mansion House, Nov. 10, 1942, Prime Minister Churchill made the following significant declaration: "We mean to hold our own. I have not become the King's First Minister in order to preside over the liquidation of the British Empire." The recent statements by Col. Oliver Stanley, British Colonial Secretary, are equally significant in this respect. Replying specifically to "a great volume of friendly criticism and disinterested advice" from the United States, Col. Stanley declared at Oxford, on March 5, 1943, that "the first and fundamental principle is that the administration of the British colonies must continue to be the sole responsibility of Great Britain." He refused to support the theory that it would benefit a particular colony or the world at large if the administration should be entrusted to "some international body." At the same time, he said, continued British administration did not exclude the possibility of "close international cooperation."[15]

[15] *New York Times,* March 6, 1943.

In the case of Burma, it is open to doubt whether Great Britain will find it easy to resume her rule over the colony, in view of the fact that the Burmese have become so extremely anti-British that they have actually committed widespread sabotage and fifth-column activities against the British defense in the course of Japanese invasion. A more rational solution seems to be, as suggested by well-informed writers, that political tutelage of Burma should be carried on not under exclusively British direction but by some international authority or agency, in which will be represented China, a neighboring country vitally interested in the future of Burma as the way of her access to the Indian Ocean, and the United States as the most powerful of the sponsors of the Atlantic Charter as well as an obviously disinterested party in respect of Burma.[16]

The ruling Power should at all events discharge its responsibility under adequate international supervision and control. No matter whether a ruling Power administers a colony in its own right or under an international mandate, the essential thing is that the administration be conducted on the basis, as well as in the spirit, of trusteeship. The exceptional case of Indo-China may require special consideration. If the Vichy regime continues its policy of collaboration with the Axis, and yet manages to survive the war, then Indo-China is likely to be taken from France entirely and put under an international administration or a mandatory regime. If a mandatory system were adopted, China, for obvious reasons, would have a good claim to the mandate.

Administration by an international commission under the authority of a regional or world organization would be the proper program for other territories in the region,

[16] See Abend, *op. cit.*, p. 173; also *Fortune, loc. cit.*, pp. 8-9.

such as the Japanese Mandated Islands. Their importance is strategic rather than economic or political, and they have no possible chance of ever standing by themselves because of their size, the sparseness of their population and a variety of other circumstances.

As a general solution of the colonial problems, international administration today seems less favored. The whole problem was thoroughly discussed at the Mont Tremblant Conference of the Institute of Pacific Relations. But no support was then found for the view that the problem could be met by the colonial Powers surrendering their administrative and financial responsibility for the area concerned, to an international authority in which sovereignty would henceforth be vested. Apart from practical difficulties, such as the complete break with tradition, the lack of any international authority with administrative experience and other requisite knowledge, it was pointed out, the colonial peoples concerned, and particularly those who feel that they are on the point of attaining independent status, would not welcome such a transfer of allegiance.[17]

The trusteeship principle in respect of colonial government seems to have had wide acceptance. At the Mont Tremblant Conference, considerable agreement was reached on the application of this principle in the treatment of colonies and subject peoples in the Pacific region. "There was general agreement that the basic policy in the parts of the world at present in colonial or dependent status must be to attain self-government at the earliest moment" and that "the time in which self-government can be attained must vary for different peoples." "The colonial nations accept, on the one hand, a trusteeship which most of them have recognized in the past towards

[17] *War and Peace in the Pacific*, p. 56.

the subject peoples, and, on the other hand, a steward-
ship in behalf of the world at large. This implies both
rights and responsibilities for the other nations, especially
for the large Powers. They would have both the right
and the duty to supervise, through a suitable agency, the
progress toward that political objective. And, to fulfill
its purpose, such an agency must inevitably also concern
itself with the social and economic welfare of these peoples
in its broad aspects." For the purpose of supervision, an
international agency or authority was actually proposed in
the form of a "regional council," which would be composed of representatives of the colonial Powers directly
concerned, of the indigenous peoples of the region, and
of independent powers without territorial interests in the
region, such as the United States, China and the U.S.S.R.
The function of this international agency, it was suggested, would in the main "comprise (a) the reception,
study and publication of periodical reports on the political, economic and social progress made in the various
areas; (b) inspection and investigation on the spot, both
on its own initiative and on the receipt of grievance from
any indigenous group; (c) the suggestion of general lines
of policy for the development of self-governing institutions as well as improvements in such matters as public
health, nutrition, landownership, working conditions,
inter-regional migration and education."[18] It was rightly
pointed out that "acceptance by the United Nations of the
principles here put forward and the immediate creation
of the agency in a preliminary form would have the effect
of spurring the war effort and of lessening the possibili-
ties of mutual misunderstanding among the United
Nations."

[18] *Far Eastern Survey,* January 11, 1943, pp. 6-7; also *War and Peace in
the Pacific,* pp. 55-58.

It is noteworthy that suggestions more or less along similar lines for application of the trustee principle to non-self-governing parts of Southeast Asia and the Pacific were also made by an Australian group in a paper submitted to the Mont Tremblant Conference. Among other things, it was proposed that "a Pacific Region Development Commission be established consisting of four types of members, whose powers should include: (1) powers of inspection as well as the receipt of information; (2) the power to recommend that a particular area is fit for self-government; (3) the power to recommend that the conditions of a mandate have been so seriously and so persistently violated that a new mandatory authority must be appointed.[19]

Another racial problem may be mentioned. There are millions of Chinese living in various parts of the Pacific region, particularly in the South Seas and Southeast Asia, where for years they have engaged in trade and other peaceful activities. But in spite of the important contributions which they have made to the economic development and prosperity of the countries where they reside, they have not all acquired full political rights. In many cases they suffer from harsh and discriminatory measures imposed by local legislative or administrative authorities. The worst situation is in Thailand, where Chinese residents have been oppressed in various ways by the Thai Government.[20] A number of anti-Chinese measures have

[19] See *Australia and the Pacific*, Vol. 1—Political, D. "The Atlantic Charter and the Problems of Southeast Asia and the Pacific," I.P.R., New York, pp. 63-4, Appendix III.

[20] The number of Chinese residing in Thailand has been variously estimated between 524,000 (referring to those regarded as "nationals" of China) according to the 1937 Thai census, and 3,000,000, (presumably persons of Chinese racial origin) the figure given by the *Chinese Year-Book* for 1938-39. A moderate estimate by the latest authority is 2,500,-000. For details, see the I.P.R. studies by K. P. Landon, *The Chinese in*

been taken in the fields of immigration, industry, education and politics. It was to prevent the Chinese community from seeking diplomatic protection against oppression by the local government that Thailand for many years followed a policy of non-intercourse with the Chinese government. The continued existence of such a state of affairs cannot be tolerated by China after a war in which Thailand chose to be on the side of the enemy. It would be in conformity with justice and peace to give these Chinese at least such political and civil rights as were usually guaranteed to national and racial groups under the prewar minorities treaties.

All these long-standing racial grievances, national aspirations and other political issues concerning subject peoples or national minorities in the Pacific region must be settled fairly in the postwar political reconstruction. If this is not done, the presence of large discontented groups constantly threatening revolt will make it difficult to build up a permanent order for the region. Meanwhile, it would be well, perhaps, if the United Nations were to make an early announcement of a general policy or principle which would be applied to the postwar government of dependencies and the treatment of subject peoples and national minorities. As stated, the object would be to promote self-government and establish greater freedom. This would help to increase the enthusiasm and effort of the native peoples for the great common cause of freedom and democracy and would nullify the malicious political propaganda of the Japanese, with its specious promises of the "liberation of the Asiatic peoples from the white man's yoke." In the words of Paul van Zeeland at the 1941 conference of the International Labor

---

Thailand, New York, Oxford, 1941, pp. 21-23; and Virginia Thompson, *Thailand: the New Siam,* New York, Macmillan, 1941, pp. 321-2.

Organization in New York, "In so far as we express clearly what we shall do with our victory, we are helping to win that victory."

There have been signs of late that the political winds are beginning to blow in this direction. In his address to the nation on February 23, 1942, President Roosevelt seemed indirectly to promise postwar freedom to all the conquered and subject peoples of the Pacific region by saying that "the people of Asia know that if there is to be an honorable and decent future for any of them or for us, that future depends on victory by the United Nations over the forces of Axis enslavement." He also declared that "the Atlantic Charter applies not only to the parts of the world that border the Atlantic, but to the whole world."

As regards the *application* of the Atlantic Charter (Clause 3) to the colonial possessions, serious doubt has been raised on account of two important facts; one is that Prime Minister Churchill has made in the House of Commons an explanation equivalent to a reservation to the effect that the declaration was primarily meant for the restoration of the sovereignty, self-government and national life of the states and nations now under the Nazi yoke, and "so that is quite a separate problem from the progressive evolution of the self-governing institutions in the regions and peoples which owe allegiance to the British crown." The other is that the American Government has publicly given a guarantee to non-allied Vichy France in respect of territorial integrity of France and her Empire. Actually a declaration of the State Department was made through the United States Consul at Noumea (New Caledonia) as follows: "The policy of the Government of the United States as regards French territory has been based upon the maintenance of the integrity of France and of the French Empire, and the eventual restoration of complete independence of all French territories." At the Mont Tremblant Conference of the Institute of Pacific Relations, these controversial points received full attention, and were fairly clarified by the explanatory statements made by British and French delegates to the Conference. On the British side, it was asserted that in the British view the Atlantic Charter has no geographical limit; it is world-wide in its application; and that there are no British reservations with regard to its applicability whatsoever; the principles of the Charter refer specifically to India and Burma and the public opinion in the House of Commons and in Great Britain as a whole is irrevocably committed to its specific application after the war. In the case of American declaration regarding French dependencies, a Fighting French member interpreted it to mean that when the war is won, the first step will be in the restoration of the territories occupied to French sovereignty; thus France would have an equal right with, say, the United Kingdom, to discuss the future status of its dependent areas. The statement of the American Government was not interpreted as being inconsistent with any developing United Nations policy respecting what are now colonial areas.[21]

It is our earnest hope that Mr. Churchill's Mansion House speech and Col. Stanley's recent Oxford speech will not lead to a retrograde step in the sense that all British colonies or possessions in Asia as well as elsewhere will be returned to the exact position they occupied before the war once the victory is won.

[21] See Dennett, *op. cit.*, pp. 1-2; Julius Stone, "The Atlantic Charter and the Problems of Southeast Asia and the Pacific," in *Australia and the Pacific*, Vol. I—Political, pp. 46-7, p. 53; *War and Peace in the Pacific*, p. 74, pp. 118-23.

Empires Versus Collective Security

In a sense the problem of colonial possession is inseparable from that of general security in the Pacific. On the one hand, colonial Powers like Great Britain and the Netherlands are said to find it difficult to loosen their hold on colonial possessions unless and until they are assured of an effective system of general security being set up in the region. On the other hand, the United States, a powerful element indispensable to any effective system of general security, may not be willing to cooperate in the establishment and maintenance of any international organization for security if the colonial Powers stick to their old imperial rule over these possessions despite the principles of the Atlantic Charter. In the words of Dr. Tyler Dennett, "what the United States may be willing to contribute to the peace in the East will be largely conditioned by the kind of measures which are to be taken to liquidate the prewar colonial system."[22] It is noteworthy that those American leaders who are ardent advocates of collective security are at the same time taking a strong stand on the freedom of colonies and subject peoples on the basis of the Atlantic Charter. Mr. Sumner Welles, Under-Secretary of State, in his Arlington Memorial Day address (May 30, 1942), declared: "Our victory must bring in its train the liberation of all peoples. Discrimination between peoples because of their race, creed, or color must be abolished. The age of imperialism is ended. The right of a people to their freedom must be recognized, as the civilized world long since recognized the right of an individual to his personal freedom. The principles of the Atlantic Charter must be guaranteed to the world as a whole—in all oceans and in all continents." Later on, Vice-President Henry

[22] Dennett, *op. cit.*, p. 5.

Wallace made a similar assertion: "Those who write the peace must think of the whole world. There can be no privileged peoples."

The close relation between the freedom of subject peoples and the problem of general security was fully explored in the discussions at the Mont Tremblant Conference of the Institute of Pacific Relations. As a result, the Conference succeeded in breaking out of this seemingly vicious circle and recognized that it was a question of "simultaneous progress all along the line." If the way to break down American isolationism, as many sincere American internationalists believe, in order to secure American cooperation in a postwar system of general security is for the colonial Powers to adopt a progressive policy towards liberation of their dependencies and subject peoples, the establishment of an organization for general security will evidently encourage the adoption, as well as facilitate the execution, of that policy to the good of all the parties concerned.[23] This leads us to the basic problem of regional organization in the Pacific which is discussed below.

[23] *Far Eastern Survey, loc. cit.,* p. 6; also Opening Statement by Lord Hailey, in *War and Peace in the Pacific,* pp. 4-15.

CHAPTER V

A REGIONAL ORGANIZATION FOR
THE PACIFIC

The idea of setting up some permanent machinery for assuring peace in the Pacific area is not new. Such an idea can be traced as far back as the Washington Conference 1921-22 which, after the adoption of the treaty relating to principles and policies concerning China, generally known as the Nine-Power Treaty, passed a resolution for establishing in China a "Board of Reference for Far Eastern Questions" to which any question arising in connection with the execution of the aforementioned treaty might be referred for investigation and report. That was perhaps the first international attempt to have a permanent machinery for dealing with Pacific affairs. It has been generally regretted that such a Board of Reference was never set up.

Further, in the Report of the League of Nations Commission of Enquiry (Lytton Commission) on the Sino-Japanese Dispute, which was in the main adopted by the League Assembly in its own Report on February 24, 1933, the Commission recommended among other things, the conclusion of a Sino-Japanese Treaty of Conciliation and Arbitration, Non-Aggression and Mutual Assistance, in which the U.S.S.R. might participate in part through a separate tripartite agreement. In the Commission's opinion, such a treaty "would provide for a board of conciliation, whose functions would be to assist in the solution of any difficulties as they arise between the Government of

61

China and Japan." "It would also establish an arbitration tribunal composed of persons with judicial experience and the necessary knowledge of the Far East. This tribunal would deal with any disputes between the Chinese and Japanese Governments regarding the interpretation of the declaration or of the new treaties, and with such other categories of disputes as might be specified in the treaty of conciliation." As is generally remembered, that well-meant project of peace machinery failed to materialize, since Japan flatly refused to accept the League's recommendations for the settlement of the Sino-Japanese Dispute.

As the Far Eastern crisis was assuming an increasingly dangerous aspect, threatening to involve the Pacific in a general conflagration, people became more convinced of the need of some permanent machinery for assuring a lasting peace in the Pacific region. During the past several years proposals or opinions in favor of such a set-up have been put forward by different persons in various forms. Some time before the outbreak of the Sino-Japanese war in 1937, a British Dominion statesman was already openly advocating a Pacific peace pact as a means of averting war in the region. Even among Japanese publicists the interest in a Pacific peace organization has not been lacking. Thus at the Banff Conference of the Institute of Pacific Relations in 1933, in a paper entitled *Some Considerations on the Future Reconstruction of Peace Machinery in the Pacific*, two Japanese professors advocated a Pacific regional organization with a treaty of security, non-aggression and arbitration, the principal parties of which would be China, Japan, the U. S. A., the Soviet Union, Great Britain and France,[1] although the

[1] For details, see Bruno Lasker and W. L. Holland, *Problems of the Pacific*, 1933, London and Chicago, 1934, pp. 12-13 and 441-450.

considerations on which their scheme was based were open to question.

Recent Proposals

Over two years ago, in a speech before the China Society in America, Dr. Hu Shih, Chinese Ambassador to the United States, urged the restoration and strengthening of the international order for the Pacific region as one of the basic conditions for a durable peace in the Far East. Later, in a paper (noted above) read before the annual meeting of the American Political Science Association on December 31, 1941, the same point was further stressed by him. Proposals based upon a similar viewpoint were also made by Mr. Raymond L. Buell; according to him, there should be a regional organization for the Pacific within the framework of a New World Association of Nations, and the regional machinery would consist of a regular Pacific Conference and a Pacific section of the Secretariat of the New World Association.[2]

At the Virginia Beach meeting of the Institute of Pacific Relations in December of 1939, the idea of permanent peace machinery for the Pacific also came to the minds of many members at the meeting. As recorded in the Proceedings of that meeting, some member pointed out that the Washington Conference did provide for continuing conferences. "It was also termed a tragic failure that the Board of Reference which had been provided for was not set up. It was also emphasized that some form of continuing organization should be set up to coordinate the work of postwar adjustments and to provide a means of continuing negotiations among the powers. Finally, most members appeared to feel that any future system of

[2] Raymond L. Buell, *Isolated America*, New York, 1940, pp. 369-373 and 438-440.

treaty machinery should be given "teeth" in the form of commitments by the signatories to take collective action against any nation which refused to abide by the provisions of the settlement and which resorted to unilateral force to achieve its aims.[3]

Two important studies on regional security, in addition to Professor N. Peffer's *Prerequisites to Peace in the Far East*, (now revised and incorporated in his recently published *Basis for Peace in the Far East*) have been made under the auspices of the Institute of Pacific Relations; both stand in the main for similar views as to the organization of peace in the Pacific region. One of these studies is in the form of an unpublished memorandum (written in August, 1941) by Mr. W. L. Holland on "The Far East in a New World Order."[4] The other is a book entitled *Post-War Worlds* by Professor P. E. Corbett of Canada. According to Mr. Holland's idea, the Pacific security organization would consist of three stages of groupings. It would start by first grouping the Netherlands Indies, the Philippines, Burma and British Malaya into an "Indonesian Union" which both Thailand and Indo-China would be invited to join after the war. This union would have as its executive agencies a regional defense board, a technical advisory bureau, and a joint economic council which would "coordinate the trade, industry, investment, public finance, migration and agricultural policies." Then in the next stage there would be a "Far Eastern group" to include China, Manchuria, Japan, the Indonesian Union, and India. This wider group might be called an Eastern League. As for the interests of such Pacific powers as the U.S.S.R. and the United States, these might be safe-

[3] Kate Mitchell and W. L. Holland, *Problems of the Pacific*, 1939, New York, 1940, pp. 127-28.

[4] Mr. Holland's memorandum is summarized in Corbett's *Post-War Worlds*, I.P.R., New York, 1942, pp. 73-80.

guarded by a wider Pacific Association which would embrace the United States, the U.S.S.R., Canada, Australia, New Zealand, the principal countries on the west coast of South America and all the units of the Far Eastern Group.

On the other hand, Professor Corbett doubts the necessity of the wider Pacific Association, while agreeing with Mr. Holland on the need of an Eastern League composed of China, Japan, India and the Indonesian Union. According to Professor Corbett's "tentative design for the organization of the Eastern League," China, Japan and India and the Indonesian Union should make a covenant of non-aggression, non-recognition of the results of aggression, security, arbitration and economic and social cooperation. For carrying out and enforcing the covenant, the Eastern League should establish (1) an assembly of delegates, (2) a military commission appointed by the assembly, (3) a Pacific court, (4) an economic and financial commission for the joint administration of the special economic interests of the region, (5) a commission on social legislation and administration, to devise common measures of public health, labor regulation, migration and control of injurious traffics, and (6) a secretariat.[5]

The Need for Regional Organization

The various proposals of views cited above provide ample evidence of the growing interest being taken in the

[5] Corbett, *op. cit.*, pp. 80-82. It is to be observed that the aforesaid proposals for the Pacific regional order were all formulated prior to the outbreak of the war in the Pacific initiated by Japan through her attack on Pearl Harbor and other Pacific posts. In the formulation of these schemes, the authors were probably assuming either that peace in the Far East might be arranged with Japan remaining out of the world war, or that, even though the world war with Japan's eventual entry on the Axis' side would be ended in the Axis' defeat, Japan might still be left a great power in the Pacific. But as things stand now, such assumptions are no longer valid.

establishment of a regional organization of peace for the Pacific. Many good reasons can be given in support of the idea of such regional organization. In the first place, the great variety of racial, economic and other complex problems in the Pacific require some international agency to handle them in such a way as to insure maximum co-operation and mutual understanding among the countries concerned. A regional organization would be in a position to meet the purpose. As Professor Corbett has well pointed out, "Even though the world were ready for a powerful federation of all states, the peculiar and complex problems of the Far Eastern area would require regional machinery decentralized and adapted to this particular environment. Remote control, without strong institutions constantly active on the spot, would be handicapped by distance and unfamiliarity." Secondly, it must be admitted that no covenant of non-aggression could be backed up by effective military assistance. Yet, the much-needed effective military assistance could only come forth from neighboring countries or near-by international military stations, if any. Particularly as the Far Eastern region geographically lies so remote from the Western World, it would be fatally risky for any Far Eastern country, as past experience has clearly demonstrated, to depend fully on a western-gravitated world league, for military assistance in case of external aggression. A regional organization ready to extend military assistance against aggression would be a basic requirement for building collective security in the Pacific region.

It is noteworthy that the regional principle is being advocated by Vice-President Wallace, the great American spokesman on world reconstruction in the following words: "As a practical matter, we may find that the regional principle is of considerable value in international affairs." "Purely regional problems ought to be left in regional hands." In Chinese official circles, Dr. Wang Chung-hui, formerly Minister of Foreign Affairs and now Secretary-General of the Supreme National Defence Council, also favors the creation of a regional system as an integral part of international organization for collective security. In his opinion, "the general collective security organization should be strengthened and made more effective by the establishment of three regional systems; firstly for Europe and the Atlantic; secondly, for the Western hemisphere; and thirdly for East Asia and the Pacific." An important Australian group on peace planning also envisaged the establishment of a regional organization in the Pacific within the wider framework of international political organization.[6]

Finally, it is a fairly prevalent view that within the framework of a general world organization, certain regional organizations should be set up in order to provide additional guaranty for peace and security. In fact, in the prewar world order, the system of regional pacts was already recognized in the Covenant of the League of Nations. Recent peace planning generally admits the idea of regional organization as a supplementary peace machinery. For instance, the Commission to Study the Organization of Peace (New York), in its Preliminary Report, has recognized "that there may be regional variations in any practical plan for world society" and that "the Soviet Union, the Far East, and the Near East, each constitute regions with distinctive characteristics; others may develop. While some rules of law must apply to all nations alike, in many matters variations must be pro-

---

[6] *Voice of China*, Nov. 10, 1942; Wang Chung-hui, "A Workable Collective Security System," in *China at War*, January, 1943. *Australia and the Pacific*, Vol. I—Political, p. 70.

vided within the distinctive regions." It is only too obvious that such a wide and important region as the Pacific with distinctive characteristics and complex problems of its own should have its regional organization functioning along with other regional organizations under the general rule of the world society. As a matter of fact, a regional organization might even be set up in the Pacific far ahead of any general organization of a world order, since the latter organization might require comparatively more time for its establishment in view of the probable need of a transitional period for accomplishing the immediate world-wide task of postwar reconstruction, especially in Europe.

An American authority would even go so far as to not only advocate the creation of a regional organization in the Pacific but also to predict a better support for the Pacific organization than for a world-wide organization like a re-established League. According to Dr. Tyler Dennett, "there is in the East, large though the area may be, a community of interest which affords a natural basis for regional organization; there does not yet exist in equal degree a sense of world-wide community of interest. Any effort to re-establish the League of Nations would in the United States introduce a very divisive subject at a time when national unity will be supremely important." He believes that "regional organization in the East would have better prospect not merely of initial ratification but also of enduring support than a re-established League with a capital in Europe or even in America; better support both in Asia and in the United States."[7]

It is particularly significant that in a recent speech (March 21, 1943), Prime Minister Churchill also made the suggestion of regional councils in Europe and Asia. But

[7] Dennett, op. cit.

he would have "the first practical task centered upon the creation of the Council of Europe," rather than upon that of Asia, as, according to his forecast, the war against Japan will still be raging after the war in Europe is ended.[8]

The need for a regional organization is made the more urgent by the recognition that the issue of colonial emancipation in the Pacific region at the end of the war is closely linked with the problem of general security, especially from the British point of view as referred to in the foregoing chapter.

At first sight, however, the idea of regional organization in the Pacific seems open to objection for a number of reasons. One obvious reason would be that it sounds like a realization of the Japanese idea of "Greater East Asia New Order" which was opposed by the Western democratic Powers and constituted the immediate cause of the Pacific war. But that reason no longer holds after Pearl Harbor. After her defeat and disarmament as a result of the war, Japan will no longer be in a position to dominate a regional organization in the Pacific. Nor would any other Power be able to do so, seeing that such a regional organization is devised not on the basis of domination by a single power but of cooperation among a multitude of nations interested in the region.

Another objection to a Pacific regional set-up may be that the application of the regional principle would involve to its logical extent multiplication of regional bodies in different areas of the world, and this would contribute to further confusion in world politics especially because of inter-regional conflicts whose occurrence cannot be averted. To this objection, our reply will be twofold. First, the Pacific regional organization along with other regional organizations is devised as a subordinate

[8] *New York Times,* March 22, 1943.

set-up within the framework of a world-wide organization. Any conflicts between these regional bodies would be considered a matter of world concern and be dealt with as such by the wider world organization, whose agencies will be ready to take appropriate measures to meet any serious inter-regional crisis. Second, as pointed out by Dr. Tyler Dennett, "there need arise no danger that such a regional system would come into conflict with some other regional system as in the Near East or in Europe, for certain powers, obviously Britain, Russia and the United States, would be members of all of them."[9]

A third objection would be that the establishment of a Pacific regional organization within the framework of a world-wide organization would involve overlapping of international agencies which is not only unnecessary but also confusing in effect. But this objection cannot hold either, for there is actually need of a regional organization in the Pacific, not only as an immediate agency for dealing with affairs of common interest in the region, but also for the purpose of general security which function could not be effectively performed by a world organization alone. This seeming overlapping of international agencies may not necessarily involve serious difficulties in their operations, if certain basic rules can be laid down on the relationship between the Pacific organization and the world-wide association.

In planning a regional organization in the Pacific, we have to take into account the prospect of a great shift in the balance of power in this region after the war. Any regional organization in the Pacific must be able to command great moral and political prestige as well as material force in order to act effectively in the discharge of its international responsibilities. For the purpose of gain-

[9] Dennett, *op. cit.*, p. 29.

ing sufficient moral and material strength, all the interested countries bordering on the Pacific should be included in the regional organization. Plans for a limited Far Eastern group as suggested by Mr. Holland and Professor Corbett could hardly answer the purpose. A regional organization alone could not assure peace and security for the Pacific without either the Soviet Union or the United States forming part of it. Nor would the scheme of having two organizations, a smaller Far Eastern group and a wider Pacific organization, set up side by side be a satisfactory solution, for the existence of such overlapping agencies in the same region would complicate matters so much that the whole scheme would not work either smoothly or effectively.

One can easily visualize that as a result of victory by the United Nations over the German-Italian-Japanese alliance, a victorious and fully restored China would be able to assume a leading position in East Asia just as Soviet Russia would be in the northern Pacific. On the other hand, Japan after her defeat and disarmament, and most likely with the loss of her previously acquired territories, might become a second-rate Power. Just because of that, the Japanese might become even more chauvinistic and revengeful for some time to come, so that their military status would have to be constantly under international supervision, and any aggressive activities on their part should be immediately held in check by the collective force of the region. At the same time, a sense of justice as well as general interest would require that fair consideration should be given to the legitimate economic needs and reasonable national aspirations of this island nation of some 73 million souls. In this respect, Japan might well depend upon the regional security machinery for necessary support.

It is natural that the great Anglo-American nations with their predominant air and sea power and increasing interests in the Pacific should be prepared to assume a decisive role in the building and maintaining of a permanent order in the region. Again, in the shaping of the postwar Pacific order, we cannot afford to overlook the importance of India. This great Eastern country, once given its promised political freedom, will surely have to be counted as a new political force capable of playing an important role in the new international set-up.

After Pearl Harbor, an important proposal for a Pacific regional scheme was put forward by the editors of the magazine *Fortune* in a report on "Pacific Relations" already cited. According to this plan, there should be set up an organization called the Pacific Council as an organ of the United Nations ("or of X, our international authority to be"), to be composed of all members of the United Nations whose interests directly touch the Pacific Ocean—ultimately including Japan. This Pacific Council would be the United Nations' final judicial authority on Pacific affairs. But it would lack executive authority of its own. "As long, however, as the working alliance of the United Nations lasts, its influence would undoubtedly be great." In addition, there would be a number of concrete jobs of cooperative international administration to be done in the Pacific area for which special cooperative bodies would be organized, with powers and constitutions of their own. But these special bodies would report to the Pacific Council, and be subject to its intervention on behalf of the United Nations as a whole.[10]

[10] *Fortune, loc. cit.,* p. 5. The suggestion of a somewhat different composition of the regional authority was also noted at the Mont Tremblant Conference as follows: "The civilian authority power is a body representing the United States, Russia, Great Britain, the Netherlands, China, Australia, New Zealand, Canada, France, the Philippine Islands, in time

At the Mont Tremblant Conference of the Institute of Pacific Relations in December, 1942, there was a fairly general agreement on the creation of an international machinery for regional security to be called the Regional Council. The members of the Regional Council were suggested to be as follows: China, Canada, Australia, New Zealand, Thailand, France, the Netherlands and Netherlands Indies, the United Kingdom, the United States, and the U.S.S.R., with the Philippine Commonwealth joining only after it has achieved independence. Other colonial areas would also become members upon attaining independence. Representation on the Regional Council of a member of the world security organization was considered also desirable.[11]

The Regional Council would have, apart from its specific responsibility in relation to the Southeast Asia colonial areas as envisaged in the previous chapter, the following three major functions: (1) the creating of conditions in which irritants to the security of the region would not arise, in other words, the task of establishing and maintaining the conditions of peace; (2) the resolving of disputes at their source and as soon as they arise, which implies a system of conciliation and arbitration; (3) the employment of force, the exercise of police power, which requires the maintenance of an armed force under inter-

India, and some day, we should hope, Japan," *War and Peace in the Pacific,* p. 79. It is to be observed that in one respect a discrepancy exists between the above suggestions on the composition of the regional organization and those in connection with the Southeast Asia colonial areas as referred in the foregoing chapter which proposed the inclusion of representatives of the indigenous peoples of the region. However, the discrepancy is considered to be probably "more apparent than real and susceptible of adjustment," *ibid.,* p. 84.

[11] *War and Peace in the Pacific,* pp. 82-84.

national authority. These post-Pearl Harbor proposals were of course formulated by taking into account the probable political changes in the Pacific after Japan's defeat. But much was left to be elaborated in detail.

Outline of a Regional Organization

Four basic problems at least must be given consideration in any planning for a regional organization of the Pacific area. First, what countries should be members of such an organization? Second, what functions should it have? Third, what agencies should be set up to carry out those functions? Fourth, what should be its relation to a world wide organization?

The first problem is simple. The membership of the organization, which might be called the Pacific Association of Nations, should include China, Soviet Russia, India, the United States, Canada, Australia, New Zealand, the Philippines, Great Britain, the Netherlands, Japan and Thailand. Japan and Thailand, however, should not be admitted to membership until after peace has been concluded and until the other member nations have satisfied themselves that their former enemies are able and willing to fulfill their duties. Should Korea recover her national freedom, as she will do unless the United Nations betray their common cause, she would certainly be entitled to membership. New members should be admitted by agreement of two-thirds of the original member nations.

The proper functions of the Pacific Association may be grouped in two distinct but related categories.

Since its main object would be to assure peace and security in the region, its chief functions naturally should be to avert war by exercising joint influence or taking joint preventive measures, and, in case war does occur, to help the victim and to enforce sanctions against the aggressor.

First of all, the member nations of the Association should bind themselves by a pact of non-aggression, arbitration and mutual assistance. Disputes between them should be submitted to arbitration, judicial decision or conciliation. Any act of war by one member against another should be met immediately by collective economic or military sanctions. A permanent international military force should be formed and placed under the control of the organization. Each member nation should contribute a definite quota to this force, which should be stationed permanently in strategic posts and be held in readiness to move anywhere within the region in case of emergency. Economic and military sanctions of the regional organization might be reinforced by the cooperation and support of a wider world organization, should one come into being. After a regional system of general security is established, the regional organization, taking account of the world armament situation, should adopt a regional plan for the reduction and limitation of armaments.

The association should also perform certain positive functions, for peace can be lasting only if it is constructive. The association therefore should promote such progressive measures as the common interests of the region require. In economic and social matters, member nations should be obligated to cooperate through international agencies. Problems related to trade opportunities, raw materials and immigration,[12] which are peculiarly compli-

[12] The racial problem in the Pacific where various races of different creeds are living side by side will become the more acute as nationalism and self-government advance further and further in this region, because the growth of nationalism and self-government often brings about a growth of interracial hostility and animosity. In the interest of peace, therefore, appropriate arrangements should be made not only for guaranteeing minority rights to those people actually living in the area but

cated in this region, should be solved in accordance with the principles of equality and reciprocity, due consideration being given to the national interests of others as well as to the legitimate needs of the countries concerned. Both in the interests of the native peoples and for the sake of peace, the Association should supervise and control the administration of colonies and dependencies in the region. Member nations should have the right to present any proposal or grievance to the Association for discussion and investigation.

To carry out its various functions the Pacific Association should be provided with the following agencies:

1. A General Conference, composed of representatives of the member nations, meeting regularly once a year and, if necessary, in extraordinary session. It should have power to discuss and decide upon policies and problems of general interest to the region as well as controversial issues between member nations.

2. A Pacific Council, composed of five members elected at the annual General Conference for a term of one year. It should have the duty of seeing that the decisions and resolutions of the General Conference are carried out by the appropriate agencies. It should also take any action that might be deemed wise and effectual to meet an emergency or crisis during the recess of the General Conference.

3. A Pacific Court, composed of from five to seven judges elected by the General Conference for a term of five years from a list of jurists to be recommended in equal number by each of the member nations. This court should

---

also for admitting new immigrants on an equitable and practical basis. A non-discriminatory annual quota system, as suggested by some writers, may be adopted as a reasonable solution for the problem of intra-Pacific migration. See *Fortune, loc. cit.,* pp. 9-10.

have compulsory jurisdiction over all justifiable disputes. It should also be competent to deal with any other matter referred to it by the parties concerned or by the General Conference or the Pacific Council. The Pacific Court might be dispensed with should a World Court be established.

4. An International Military Staff, appointed by the General Conference. It should command an international force and should, if necessary, formulate and execute military sanctions under the authority of the General Conference or of the Pacific Council during the recess of the Conference.

5. A Permanent Secretariat, appointed by the Council with the approval of the General Conference and acting under the general direction of both these bodies. It should serve as an information and research center on the economic, social and other problems of the region.

Member nations should not be represented equally in the General Conference. The relative sizes of the delegations might be fixed according to the areas and populations of the respective countries, their economic resources and other political or cultural factors.

A unanimous vote should not be required to make a decision of the Conference or the Council valid. In both cases a two-thirds majority should suffice. The necessity of unanimity would seriously handicap the organization in taking effective action in a crisis; on the other hand, decision by a simple majority would be too risky, in view of the gravity and importance of the issues which might be involved.[13]

[13] At the Mont Tremblant Conference the question of how the Regional Council is to reach decisions has been discussed. There was agreement that no questions should require unanimity. Some types of questions might be determined by a mere majority, others by a two-thirds vote, *War and Peace in the Pacific*, p. 84.

The General Conference should meet in extraordinary session at the request of a majority of the member nations or on the initiative of the Council. The Council should be required to submit regular reports to the meetings of the General Conference and should be responsible to the Conference for the discharge of its duties.

Each member nation should be entitled to put forward a candidate for election to the Council by the General Conference, but not more than one person of the same nationality should be eligible for membership on the Council or the Pacific Court at the same time. This would prevent any single nation from dominating either of these basic institutions of the Association. The organization of the International Military Staff and the Permanent Secretariat would present more delicate problems and would probably require more elaborate planning. But the basic principle to be followed can be stated simply: these executive agencies should be so organized as to insure professional competence and efficiency as well as loyalty to the Association.

The seat of the Pacific Association should be at an internationalized place where the Secretariat, the Pacific Court and the International Military Staff could be located permanently. Meetings of the General Conference and the Council should be held at this place or at such other places as might be selected on occasion. A rational solution of the problem of financing the organization would be to divide its cost among the member nations in proportion to the number of representatives allotted to each in the General Conference.

An International Regional Police Force

Since an international force would constitute a most vital part of the regional system of general security, it requires careful planning for its organization. National quotas to the international force may be furnished in the form of monetary contributions, recruits and weapons, or in actual contingents, according as this force is to be a special military formation under international authority or just a conglomeration of national armed units. From the point of view of military efficiency as well as unified allegiance, probably a properly internationally organized force will answer better the purpose.[14] It is to be noted that at the Mont Tremblant Conference, in the discussion of the regional machinery for general security, the importance of having an international armed force was also stressed. There was some difference of opinion as to whether the force should be completely internationalized as a mercenary force actually belonging to the regional council through financial contributions made by its members, or whether the force should be composed of armed units still belonging to the respective members of the Council but loaned to it under agreed quotas. There was, according to the report of the Conference, a majority in favor of the former.[15]

A major part of the international force will necessarily consist of air force, which is expected to play a decisive role in international action to curb aggression. Naturally there will be need for a series of air bases strategically situated both on the mainland and on the islands spread over the Pacific region. In this connection, however, proposals by various writers for the establishment of the so-called "chain of bases," "security lines of naval and air bases," "trans-Pacific defence belt," "trans-Pacific chain of

[14] In Mr. Ely Culbertson's World Federation Plan, formation of an international mobile corps is devised more or less along this line. Ely Culbertson, *Summary of the World Federation Plan,* New York, 1943, pp. 35-36.

[15] *War and Peace in the Pacific,* pp. 83-84.

fortified islands," or whatever else one may call it, requires serious examination.[16]

It is to be observed that the armed force to be used in the event of aggression must necessarily vary both in scope and in nature at different stages of the crisis. As a permanent means of maintaining security the international force will have to hold itself ready to come to the prompt rescue of the victim as well as to hold the aggressor in check in the initial stage of any aggression. In ordinary case, this will probably be sufficient to accomplish its end by warding off immediate danger. But in case of the crisis assuming such a dangerous aspect as to involve a major war, the assistance and cooperation of national forces will have to be called for. From this consideration two important conclusions can be drawn: first, the regional international force need not be very large; second, this force does not mean to provide a substitute for the national armed forces of member-nations of the regional organization, although an eventual limitation and reduction of national armaments, as envisaged above, should be adopted by the international authority in the region.

Relation of a Pacific to a World Organization

The regional organization in the Pacific should be started immediately at the end of the war, regardless of whether there is a long period of armistice or whether a world organization is set up simultaneously. If a wider world organization does come into existence, the Pacific Association, like other regional organizations, should be subordinated to the more inclusive body. At the same time, the world organization could coordinate the related

[16] George W. Keeton, *Some Factors in A Far Eastern Peace Settlement*, p. 22; Royal Institute of International Affairs, *Problems of Postwar Settlement in the Far East, A Preliminary Survey*, p. 12; *Fortune, loc. cit.*, pp. 11-12.

activities of the regional organizations and extend to them any aid which might be necessary. Thus the Pacific Association would in the long run gain moral and material strength from the world organization.

No hard and fast rules can be laid down regarding the exact relationship between the regional organization and the world organization; much would depend upon the character and scope of the latter. Observance of one simple principle might, however, avert serious conflicts of jurisdiction and ensure better coordination of the common efforts of the two organizations. Matters of purely local concern should be left entirely in the hands of the regional organization except for such special advice and assistance as it might formally request. Regarding matters which by their nature tend to affect the interests of the world as a whole, such as access to key raw materials, problems of national or racial freedom, and sanctions against aggressors, the world organization should have the last word. Before taking any decisive action on such questions, therefore, the Pacific Association should, except for necessary precautionary measures, seek the approval and cooperation of the world organization.

CHAPTER VI

CHINA AS A STABILIZING FACTOR IN A NEW WORLD ORDER

Now that we have a fairly clear idea of what a postwar order in the Pacific might mean, we may examine China's position in the new order.

Chinese Future Foreign Policy

First of all, the Western democracies need not fear that China will ever become too strong. The Chinese are essentially a peace-loving people who would never deliberately make war on other nations with a view to securing territorial expansion or political dominance. On the contrary, a free, strong, prosperous, and democratic China would serve as the greatest stabilizing factor of a new order in the Pacific region. Such a remark would be superfluous but for the fact, pointed out by Professor Johnstone, that there are actually in America people who fear "this new China will develop aggressive tendencies that can be kept in check only by a strong Japan, a strong Russia, and a United States willing and able to exercise its power across the Pacific."[1] For that reason, these people would not only advocate the maintenance of a strong Japan after the war, but some of them even would keep Japan in Manchuria and Korea as well.[2]

[1] William C. Johnstone, "Must We Keep Japan Strong?", *Far Eastern Survey*, November 2, 1942.

[2] E.g. Professor N. J. Spykman, in his geopolitical treatise, *America's Strategy in World Politics*. Mr. Hugh Byas in his book *Government by*

The fear of China becoming too strong and aggressive after the war is itself an exaggeration and will not be borne out by the facts. No doubt, after the victory is won, China will, as she must, be strong in her national defense against foreign aggression. But with her limited capacity for heavy industry development, it would be scores of years before China could build up a scale of armament strong enough to conduct an offensive war for the purpose of aggression. From the viewpoint of political strategy, the idea of keeping Japan strong in order to balance the potential power of China comes to the same thing as what the Chinese characterize as "drinking poison to quench thirst"—an almost criminally stupid way of meeting a need. For the purpose of guarding against any potential aggressive power in the postwar Pacific, be it China, Russia, Japan or whoever else, would it not be much safer as well as more effective to rely upon a system of collective security based on a regional organization, as outlined in the previous chapter of this book, than to resort to the antiquated practice of balance of power?

The fact that China cherishes no designs of territorial expansion beyond her original frontiers has been already made clear by both Generalissimo Chiang Kai-shek and Foreign Minister T. V. Soong in their recent statements. In his address at the closing ceremony of the first Plenary Session of the Third People's Political Council in Chungking, on October 31, 1942, the Generalissimo made the following important declaration regarding China's war aims: "We have been fighting this war of resistance with

Assassination, advocates stripping Japan of all its conquests, including Manchuria but not Korea. It seems he has also a revival of balance of power in view. Possibly those who propose internationalization or an Anglo-American control of the wholly Chinese island of Formosa are also motivated by the same consideration of a balance of power. See *Fortune loc. cit.*

purity of motive and consistency of principle—not for any selfish purpose but for the salvation of the world through first saving ourselves. Towards Asia as towards the whole world we wish only to do our duty to the exclusion of any lust for power or other desires incompatible with the moral dictates of love and benevolence that are characteristic of the Chinese national spirit. The aim of the Revolution is, so far as the interests of China herself are concerned, the restoration of her original frontiers and, in regard to the rest of the world, a gradual advance of all nations from the stage of equality to that of an ideal unity."[3]

At the press conference in Chungking, on November 3, Dr. Soong stressed the same point of view regarding China's territorial aims at the end of the war by saying that "we will get back Manchuria, Formosa, and the Liuch'iu Islands; we have no territorial aspirations beyond what is rightfully ours; the Generalissimo at the People's Political Council refuted the idea that China aspires to be the leader of Asia because the 'Fuehrer' principle implies domination."[4] If these statements represent, as they should, China's official attitude towards postwar world settlement, there can be no ground for the apprehension that a strong new China would tend to embark upon a policy of aggression to the detriment of the national security of neighboring nations as well as of the general interests of world peace.

With the end of the unequal treaties and a successful settlement of other long-standing issues between China and foreign powers, a new era will begin in the history of China's relationship with foreign powers. Once she

---

[3] *Voice of China*, November 3, 1942.

[4] *Voice of China*, November 5, 1942. See also *New York Herald-Tribune*, November 4, 1942 (UP dispatch from Chungking, November 3).

has successfully vindicated her legitimate claim for freedom and equality in the family of nations, China will have no further quarrel with Western powers over any old issue, but instead will be in a position to promote better economic and cultural relations as well as political cooperation with other nations.

The chief cause of this anxiety seems to lie in the possibility of a clash of interests between China and Russia in the north as well as between her and Great Britain in the south as visualized by Dr. Tyler Dennett.[5] It is apparent that there may be such a potential danger in the Far East, but with good will and statesmanship on both sides, this can and must be averted through some long-term understanding.

Relations with Britain

In Southeast Asia, the conflicts of interests between China and Britain are supposed to be most likely to arise. But here China's position can easily be clarified. As a matter of general principle, China simply stands for an early ending of the imperialism of the old order in this region. As far as her own interests are concerned, China will see to it that in the postwar settlement, special consideration be given to (1) peace and security of her southern frontiers, (2) security of land passages to the South Seas, (3) protection of the economic interests as well as minority rights of the Chinese resident in the region. There will be only two outstanding territorial issues to be settled; Hongkong and Macao. Macao, a tiny place on the South China coast, has been under Portuguese occupation as a trading post for more than three hundred

[5] "On the contrary, conflicts of interests are bound to develop: possibly between China and Russia; also certainly between China and Britain." Dennett, *op. cit.*

years. But it was only in the latter part of the last century that China formally confirmed "perpetual occupation and government of Macao and its dependencies by Portugal."[6] Morally as well as materially, Portugal would hardly be in a position to stand in the way of China getting back Macao, Portuguese rule over which not only infringes China's territorial integrity, but also disgraces Western civilization by presenting a Monte Carlo of an even worse type in the Far East.[7] As for Hongkong, which will no longer be very useful as a British strategic outpost in the Far East, it seems the British Government could well afford to rectify a century-old wrong done to China by returning this island immediately after the war as a token of mutual friendship and confidence between the two great nations and allies in the war. Rendition of British sovereignty over Hongkong, however, could not be accepted by China as a price for giving up her claim over Formosa in favor of international sovereignty as suggested by some writers. It is all the more important that an early agreement on the return of Hongkong to China should be reached, in view of the fact that Great Britain is apt to link the question of Kowloon with that of Hongkong. From the British point of view, "Hongkong is peculiar because, while the whole area was a British colony, one part of it was ceded as a result of the two Anglo-Chinese wars in the 19th century and the other portion was only leased for a term of years which still has fifty-five years to run."[8] Hongkong was considered indefensible without the

[6] Protocol of Lisbon, 26th March, 1887. The Protocol explicitly obligates Portugal "never to alienate Macao and dependencies without agreement with China."

[7] See Hallett Abend, *Pacific Charter*, pp. 67-70.

[8] By the Treaty of Nanking, 29th August, 1842, China ceded to Great Britain the Island of Hongkong. Later by the Treaty of Peking, 24th October, 1860, China further ceded to Great Britain, to have and to hold, as a dependency of H. M.'s Colony of Hongkong, "that portion

protection of defensive works on the Kowloon peninsula across the bay, and what is more, "the two portions of the colony form a single economic unit and one could hardly be administered if cut off from the other."[9] For this reason, the British Delegation at the Washington Conference of 1921-2 made an exception of Kowloon in the declaration of British policy in favor of returning leased territories to Chinese administration; and obviously for the same reason the British Government again declined to discuss the question of Kowloon during the recent negotiations for relinquishing British extraterritorial rights in China.[10] It seems, therefore, that an early settlement of the fundamental issue of Hongkong is bound up with the termination of the lease of Kowloon territory. Of course, in return for this important friendly gesture on the part of Britain, the Chinese nation would surely be generous enough to give consideration to legitimate British rights and economic interests in Hongkong in detailed arrangements concerning the settlement.

It is hard for Chinese to accept the view, as advanced

---

of Township of Kowloon" which was leased to Mr. Harry Smith Parkes. Finally an extension of Hongkong territory was further effected on the side of Kowloon under lease by the Sino-British Agreement of Peking, (9th June, 1898) in the following terms: "Whereas it has for many years past been recognized that an extension of Hongkong territory is necessary for the proper defense and protection of the Colony. It has now been agreed between the Governments of Great Britain and China that the limits of British Territory shall be enlarged under lease to the extent indicated generally on the annexed map. The term of the lease shall be 99 years."

[9] See the opening statement by Lord Hailey, in *War and Peace in the Pacific*, p. 6; also *Problems of Post-War Settlement in the Far East, A Preliminary Survey*, p. 2; Keeton, *op. cit.*, p. 18.

[10] At a press conference in Chungking, Dr. T. V. Soong, Minister of Foreign Affairs, revealed that China broached the question of the Kowloon leased territory but the British Government was not prepared to discuss the question. The Foreign Minister later said that China reserved the right to raise the question again. The question of Hongkong, he added, was never brought up. *Voice of China*, January 13, 1943.

by a Briton of outstanding authority, that "it will not be possible to regard the future of Hongkong to be determined merely by bargaining between the United Kingdom and China on the basis of old standing treaty rights"; and that "the future of Hongkong must depend on the general settlement to be made between China and the members of the Pacific group" as to the provisions of key points to be maintained for purposes of security and for the continuance of transit trade.[11] This would make the issue more complicated as well as involve further delay in its settlement. What the Chinese expect of Great Britain in respect of Hongkong is a simple and immediate agreement to its retrocession to China. As for matters of international concern in Hongkong—such as security bases, trade facilities which might, as one could visualize, require a general settlement—they could be left to negotiation after the restoration of Chinese sovereignty over the island.

On the whole, however, there is nothing fundamentally irreconcilable between China and Great Britain in regard to either their national interests or their world outlook. What is much needed is sufficient mutual understanding and mutual respect between the two great allied nations to assure the peace as well as win the war.

Relations with Soviet Russia

As for China's relations with Soviet Russia after the war, it is generally felt that there are three dangerous factors to be seriously considered. In the first place, between China and Russia there lies such an exceptionally long land frontier that the problem of preventing occurrence of frontier incidents and of adequately defending

[11] Opening Statement by Lord Hailey, in *War and Peace in the Pacific*, p. 6.

the frontier will be very hard to tackle on both sides. Second, the outstanding territorial issue of Outer Mongolia will remain a cause of disagreement between the two nations. Third, there will be apprehension or suspicion on China's part if Soviet Russia gives active support, political or material, to the Chinese Communist Party in opposition to the Chinese National Government.

Nevertheless, it is quite possible that these two great neighboring and friendly nations may, through mutual understanding and respect, find a way of averting any dangerous conflict of interests between them. It seems the third factor would not constitute a serious problem after the war, in view of the fact that Soviet policy under the direction of Stalin has been so far consistent in not interfering with Chinese domestic affairs, i.e. by refraining from giving direct support to the Chinese Communist movement as against the National Government. There is ample ground for the hope that after the war the Soviet Union will continue such a non-interference policy. A victorious China under a unified and strengthened National Government will be able to deal with the Communist problem in a more effective and democratic way with a view to insuring national unity as well as social progress of the Republic. It would seem that the dissolution of the Third International as recently announced in Moscow should help to simplify the Communist problem in post-war China, so far as its international aspect is concerned.

The question of Outer Mongolia is not insoluble either. On the one hand, Soviet Russia seems to have disclaimed any territorial design on that part of Chinese territory. In the note addressed on April 9, 1936, to the Chinese Government in reply to the latter's note of protest against the signing (March 12, 1936) of the Protocol of Mutual Assistance between U.S.S.R. and Outer Mongolia, the Soviet Union declared the Protocol did not "admit of or contain any territorial claims by the U.S.S.R. in regards to China or the Mongolian Republic" and that the Soviet Government "confirmed once more that the Sino-Soviet Agreement of 1924 as far as the U.S.S.R. is concerned remained in force in future." Thus the Soviet Government re-affirmed unreservedly its recognition of Outer Mongolia as an integral part of China and its respect for Chinese sovereignty therein.[12] On the other hand, oppression or forced assimilation will not be, and indeed has never been, China's policy toward racial minorities within her border. After the war is won Russia will no longer have any fear of the Japanese menace on the Siberian border. Then there would be no reason why the Soviet Government could not withdraw Soviet troops from Outer Mongolia, while China would deem it wise and safe to grant the Outer Mongolian people, if they desire, a regime of self-government compatible with Chinese sovereignty.

This question is closely related to the problem of the security of the land frontier between China and Russia. In a long range view, this problem has to be solved in terms of general peace and security. The essential thing is that there should be some long-term arrangement capable of establishing such mutual confidence that it would be considered unnecessary to guard the whole line of the frontier with large military forces. A mutual pledge of non-aggression with the subsequent demilitarization of the frontier zone would go a long way towards insuring permanent peaceful good-neighbor relations between the two nations. Such a view has been expressed with deep conviction by Dr. Hu Shih in the following words: "It is my sincere hope that the time will soon come when

[12] See *Chinese Year Book 1936-7*, p. 427.

China and the Soviet Union may work shoulder to shoulder not only in fighting a common foe, but in all time to come, with a common frontier extending nearly five thousand miles, China and Russia should work out a permanent scheme of peace, non-aggression, mutual assistance, and general security, somewhat along the same lines as the latest British-Soviet Treaty. The historical example of 3,500 miles of undefended common frontier between Canada and the United States can be emulated by China and Russia to our mutual benefit. The peace and prosperity of Asia demand such a mutual understanding between these two great countries which comprise three-quarters of the continent.[13]

China's Constructive Role

What specific, positive part could a victorious and fully-restored China, freed from all juridical and extraterritorial restrictions and from foreign economic and political dominance, play in the new Pacific order?

In the first place, China could lead the way to democracy in Asia. After she has won the war in close association with the Western democracies, China will most likely direct her political reconstruction towards the goal of constitutional democracy. A successful inauguration of political democracy in a country of 450 million people and possessing an ancient and distinguished civilization could not fail to have a tremendous effect on the political trends of other Asiatic countries.

Secondly, China could use her growing influence, moral as well as political, to help build a better order in the Pacific. No one can deny that a free China, with growing power and yet maintaining its old traditions of peace, would be a great moral force for peace and justice

[13] Hu Shih, *op. cit.*

throughout the whole region. Especially would this be true if China were able to cooperate with a free India, whose people have manifested a striking confidence in the Chinese people as well as warm friendship for them. Further, China could help to assure a progressive and orderly development of political life in the Pacific region by exercising a moderating influence on the postwar relations between the Western powers and the Asiatic peoples who aspire to be free from foreign rule.

Thirdly, from the military point of view, China could make an important contribution to the enforcement of peace. A victorious China must be made militarily strong for defense. Because of her great resources in man power, as well as because of her geographic position, a strong China could share with other Great Powers the responsibility of policing the Pacific region and enforcing sanctions against would-be aggressors. In fact, China would be one of the few Great Powers which could play an effective military role in the region.

Thus in all respects the permanent order in the Pacific will depend considerably upon the part which China is enabled to play after the war has been won by the United Nations. In the struggle for a position of full equality and freedom the Chinese nation must of course be conscious of the truth, as foreign friends would point out, that "the traffic cannot be only one way." China will undoubtedly be ready to contribute her proper share in the building up of a general system of security in the Far East. The question is often asked in this connection; "What, however, of China's own contribution to the requirements of security?" China, it is said, "will have to bear her part in the provision of the key places which the needs of common security demand," and "a critical question will arise in particular as to the position of

Formosa in this respect." It is in this direction, one would emphasize, it is essential that China "should make her own contribution to our common purpose."[14] This involves the whole fundamental issue of the need of the so-called "chain of bases," or "trans-Pacific defence belt" under a system of Pacific region security as outlined in the foregoing chapter. As far as China is concerned, assuming such international defence chain of bases are an essential requirement for the maintenance of Pacific security, she would certainly consent to the use of strategically situated portions of her territory such as Formosa and Hongkong as international bases. However, it cannot be too much emphasized that such consent on the part of China will be given only on the following conditions: first, China's territorial sovereignty over the said territory will not be sacrificed because of the establishment of an international base thereon; second, the whole arrangement must be made on the basis of equality and reciprocity in the sense that other powers of the United Nations are equally lending strategic bases for the same international purpose; third, there must be set up an international authority, whether in the form of a regional organization as proposed above or some other international body, which can exercise effective control over the use of the international bases strictly in the interest of general security.

Finally, one essential point must be made clear. If the United Nations are really working through common effort for a permanent order in the post-war world, China for one will not shrink from playing her proper role in that new order, especially in so far as she is in a position to contribute to the furtherance of peace and general

[14] Opening Statement by Lord Hailey, in *War and Peace in the Pacific*, p. 7.

security in the Pacific region. Such an international out-look on the part of the Chinese nation is best shown in the words of Generalissimo Chiang Kai-shek who, in the message to the Chinese people and armies on the occasion of the signing of the Sino-American and Sino-British treaties for relinquishing extraterritorial rights, declared that China will "march forward with a common purpose until we can join our allies in building a better world as we have joined with one another to build a better nation."

INDEX